Ibiza Island Travel Guide, Spain

Formentera Environment, Ibiza Tourism

Author
David Mills.

SONITTEC PUBLISHING. All rights reserved. No part of this publication may be reproduced, distributed, or transmitted in any form or by any means, including photocopying, recording, or other electronic or mechanical methods, without the prior written permission of the publisher, except in the case of brief quotations embodied in critical reviews and certain other noncommercial uses permitted by copyright law. For permission requests, write to the publisher, addressed "Attention: Permissions Coordinator," at the address below.

Copyright © 2019 Sonittec Publishing
All Rights Reserved

First Printed: 2019.

Publisher:
SONITTEC LTD
College House, 2nd
Floor
17 King Edwards
Road,
Ruislip
London
HA4 7AE

Table of Content

SUMMARY 1
INTRODUCTION 4
HISTORY 8
TRAVEL INFORMATION 17
   ABOUT IBIZA 17
      Why Travel to Ibiza? 21
      Ibiza Weather 26
      Food & Drink 30
         Gastronomy 34
   ISLAND GUIDE 38
      Ibiza Town 38
      Santa Eularia d'es Riu 40
      San Antonio de Portmany, Ibiza 42
      Portinatx, Ibiza 44
   PLACES TO VISIT 45
      Ibiza Beaches 46
         Best Ibiza Beaches: Relaxing 47
         Top Ibiza Beaches: Parties 52
      Cueva de Can Marça, Ibiza 58
      Ibiza Theme & Water Parks 59
   CULTURE & THE ARTS 61
      Museums in Ibiza, Spain 61
      Ibiza Dance Music 65
      Theatre & Concert Venues in Ibiza 70
      Ibiza Holidays and Festivals 73
      Leisure Activities 86
      Cinemas in Ibiza 98
   OUT & ABOUT 100
      Ibiza Nightlife 100
         Top Ibiza Clubs 101
         Pacha Ibiza 111
         Ibiza Bars 113
         Amnesia 117
         Eden 120

- El Divino 122
- Es Paradis 125
- Privilege 127
- Space 130
- Ibiza Restaurants 133
- Ibiza Shopping 138
- Ibiza Sports.. 141
  - Tennis 142
  - Mountainbike..142
  - Golf..143
  - Horse riding...143
  - Water Sports in Ibiza 144
  - Windsurfing...144
  - Diving..145
  - Ibiza Adventure Sports..146
    - Hike in Ibiza, Spain..147
- TRIPS FROM IBIZA 148
  - Travel to Formentera.. 149
  - Travel to Mallorca... 154
  - Travel to Menorca 158
- PLANNING YOUR TRIP 162
  - Travel & Transportation... 162
    - Ibiza Airports..163
    - Cheap Flights to Ibiza...164
    - Balearic Island Ferries..166
    - Ibiza Bus Travel..168
    - Car Hire Ibiza..169
  - Ibiza Property & Real Estate.. 172
    - Spanish Mortgages 176
    - Luxury Villas in Ibiza...179
  - Spain Visas & Embassies 181
  - Health and Safety 185
  - Travel Tips 185
- IBIZA CHIC: ITS BACKGROUNDS, ITS HERITAGES, AND ITS ACTUALITIES . 188

Summary

The world is a book and those who do not travel read only one page.
It is indeed very unfortunate that some people feel traveling is a sheer waste of time, energy and money. Some also find traveling an extremely boring activity. Nevertheless, a good majority of people across the world prefer traveling, rather than staying inside the confined spaces of their homes. They love to explore new places, meet new people, and see things that they would not find in their homelands. It is this very popular attitude that has made tourism, one of the most profitable, commercial sectors in the world.

People travel for various reasons. Some travel for work, others for fun, and some for finding mental peace. Though every person may have his/her own reason to go on a journey, it is essential to note that traveling, in itself, has some inherent advantages. For one, for some days getting away from everyday routine is a pleasant change. It not only refreshes one's body, but also mind and soul. Traveling to a distant place and doing exciting things that are not thought of otherwise, can rejuvenate a person, who then returns home, ready to take on new and more difficult challenges in life and work. It makes a person forget his worries, problems, frustrations, and fears, albeit for some time. It gives him a chance to think wisely and constructively. Traveling also helps to heal; it can mend a broken heart.

For many people, traveling is a way to attain knowledge, and perhaps, a quest to find answers to their questions. For this, many people prefer to go to faraway and isolated places. For believers, it is a search for God and to gain higher knowledge; for others, it is a search for inner peace. They might or might not find what they are looking for, but such an experience certainly enriches their lives

Introduction

Hoping to escape on a sun-filled jaunt round the mediterranean? Ibiza is the place for you!

One of the smallest Balearic Islands, Ibiza is home to a rich culture which takes the best from Spain and blends it with its own unique Balearic way of life. Inland you can enjoy lushly vegetated landscapes, whilst along the coast you can explore endless sun-drenched beaches. What more could you ask for?

What many people come for is undeniably the world's most hedonistic nightlife. Between June and September every year, Ibiza accommodates vast numbers of clubbers ready to live it up in some of the most renowned dance venues ever known to man. These superclubs get bigger and better every year as they viciously compete for the best international DJ's and the most clientele. For those of you that are coming to Ibiza to dance every night away, we've got the lowdown on the top Ibiza clubs so you get exactly what you want from the island.

Ibiza's towns are fun packed places to wander around and are always buzzing with life and excitement. Several of the larger ones like Santa Eularia and San Antonio de Portmany are well maintained with lots of facilities for foreign visitors, making them especially popular with tour operators organising package trips. However, for a more authentic bit of Ibizan life, book into Ibiza Town. The island's capital constantly surprises visitors with its stunning old centre, beautifully preserved and recognised by UNESCO. This is a real unexpected treat and a million miles from the preconceived visions of Ibiza. You can also indulge in a wide range of Ibiza restaurants and sample all types of food, from fusion experimental cuisine in the island's swakiest diners, to traditional Balearic food and drink as rated by the locals. On the other hand, if you're looking to enjoy the great outdoors and a rugged, undeveloped coastline, head northwards to Portinatx, Ibiza. Here you can enjoy a wide range of outdoor activities and sports and feel truly detached from the clubber's paradise that inhabits the south of the island. Use our Ibiza guide to check out the urban hotspots on the island.

Undoubtedly, beaches are one of the main drawcards to the island and you won't be disappointed with Ibiza's extensive selection of them. Be it 24 hour partying, serious sun sizzling, family fun or a relaxed little cove that you're in the mood for they'll be an Ibiza beach to suit your needs.

The wonderful thing about Ibiza is that it is such a malleable destination, one that suits many different people. The weather is good all year round, even in winter the climate is pleasant which makes Ibiza a choice destination in low season as well as the scorching summer months. If you're looking for an affordable Christmas break then take advantage of Ibiza's reduced winter tariffs rather than looking to more expensive destinations.

Whatever you're hoping to see or do on the 'White Island', our Ibiza Guide has got it covered, so dive in and explore the beautiful island of Ibiza!

History

Recent archaeological diggings prove that the first settlements on Ibiza and Formentera date back to over 3000 years ago. A grave was found on Formentera which dates back to 1600 years B.C. Cave paintings at Ses Fontanelles (north from San Antonio 800 years B.C.) and bronze axes and discs found near San Juan and San Agustin (700 years B.C.) provide further evidence of these early settlements.

The Carthaginians

In the year 654 B.C. the Carthaginians discovered Ibiza and founded Ibiza Town, making this one of the earliest towns in Europe. The christened the town *Ibossim*, quite similar to its present day name. Another name for Ibiza which has survived until now comes from the Greeks, who came to Ibiza during the time of the Carthaginians: they called the two islands of Ibiza and Formentera, the *Pitiusas* which means the pine-covered island.

The history of Formentera

The Carthaginian people originated in *Phoenicia*, and became known as the Carthaginians after the founding of the city of Carthage (geographically located in the Tunisia of today). Whilst the Romans called them in Latin, the *Punic* folk.

The Carthaginians were merchants and traders, and Ibiza became a very important trading centre. Even in those days, Ibiza boasted a large harbour and strong city walls (although the walls we can see today were built much, much later). The most important of the goods traded was 'White Gold'

Salt. The Salinas which were constructed by the Carthaginians are still used to day to win salt from sea water, by a process of evaporation.

Ibiza also played an important role in the Carthaginian culture as their largest burial grounds. Historians assume that the dead were buried here because there were no wild animals to dig them out again. The burial grounds at *Puig des Molins* in Ibiza Town is home to the world's largest collection of punic artefacts most of which have been discovered in graves. A case of the dead being buried with utensils and objects to help them on the way in the next life.

Amongst the Gods of the Carthaginians, the Goddess Tanit enjoys particular fame. She is the Mother of the Gods, the Goddess of the Earth and of fertility. You can see her image on many of the ceramic pots made on Ibiza today.

The Romans

'Carthage must be destroyed'. It was this battle cry which accompanied the Romans into the Punic Wars. They succeeded, and eventually, in 123 B.C., conquered the Balearic Islands. Not even Hannibal could prevent this, when he marched across the Alps with his elephants 100 years previously to invade and conquer Rome, (which, as you may know, he didn't quite manage). This legendary general is supposed to have been born on the island of *Conejera* just off the coast of San Antonio.

The Romans called Ibiza, *Ebusus*. The island was not however made part of the Roman Empire. It retained its independence as a confederation town. Evidence of the Roman occupation can still be seen by the gates at the entrance to Dalt Vila (the Old Town), where there are two copies of Roman statues; and in Santa Eulalia, where the old Roman bridge crosses the now dried-up river at the entrance to the town. This bridge has recently been restored.

After the Romans, between the 5th and 9th centuries A.D. there are large gaps in the chronological history of the Pitiusan Islands. Remember that this is the time of the Goths and Visigoths in Europe a dark ages where there is little historical record. During this time, Ibiza was invaded and conquered by such folk as the Vandals, the Barbarians and the Byzantines. Ibiza enjoyed a certain independence under the Byzantine Empire. Improvements to her irrigation system and the share-cropping system are due to Byzantine influence. One of the few relics of this epoch is the underground Chapel at Santa Ines.

The Arabs
The Arabs came in the 9th century A.D. and stayed for almost 500 years. They called the island

Yebisah. The arabic influence can still be felt strongly today in many customs, such as the construction of the houses, traditional costumes and musical instruments, and of course in the island dialect 'Ibicenco'.

On the hill in Ibiza Town, they built a large mosque (on the ruins of a temple dedicated to the God Mercury) and fortified the city walls. The remains of these walls and some of the watchtowers can still be seen today. Ibiza experienced a period of economic growth under Arab rule. The Salt fields, agriculture and fishing were the main sources of income.

The Catalans

Ibiza was conquered by the Catalans on the 8th August, 1235. Legend says that the the strongly fortified citadel was only eventually captured through treachery: Ibiza Town was considered at that time to be unconquerable due to its city walls and fortuitous geographical location. However, the ruling Sheik and his brother quarrelled over a mistress from his harem, whereupon the brother revealed the secret underground entrance to the Town, to the besieging Catalan forces. You can still see this secret passage in the *Calle de San Ciriaco* in Dalt Vila. Unfortunately you can't crawl through it, as it is fenced off to the public!

The Churches

The Catalans tore down the Arab mosque, and built the present day Cathedral on its foundations. The villages of the island were renamed after Christian Saints, and many churches were constructed: the oldest of which are in Santa Eulalia, San Antonio, San Miguel and Sant Jordi. Most of the rest of the island's churches were built in the 18th century.

The medieval festival is held every year on the second Friday in May. Come and see how we lived in Ibiza 1000 years ago!

The Pirates

The ruling Catalans (from mainland Spain) rather neglected the islands during the following centuries, which were marked by plundering and marauding by pirates. In order to defend themselves, the villagers built the defensive churches with extra fortified walls, where the village would shelter in the event of an attack. These churches often had cannons on their roofs! In the 16th century, the Italian architect Calvi completed the construction of the walls of Ibiza Town the same walls we see today.

The pirate towers lining the coast were built a bit later. Some of them can still be seen today. Originally, each of these towers was within sight of the next one. In the event of an invasion or sighting of a pirate ship, the tower would light a warning fire, which could be seen by the next tower, which in turn lit its own fire, and so on, until the the entire island was aware of the danger, and was able to seek safety in the churches. A primitive but very effective early warning system.

Ibiza today is perhaps not so different. People from many races and countries descend upon the island each year, take what they want and depart. The locals have been used to this type of behaviour for thousands of years. No wonder that the islanders are famous for their tolerance!

Travel Information

About Ibiza

Ibiza, the third largest of the Balearic Islands, is located in the Mediterranean Sea only 79 km (49 mi) off the coast of the Northeastern Spanish city of Valencia. With 40 km (24 mi) of sandy beaches, crystal clear water and an pleasant temperature all year round, Ibiza is a popular tourist destination in Spain. The unique environment and varied cultures in Ibiza make the island known all over the world for its vitality and diversified night life. However, the island also lays claim to a long and significant history as well as a crucial environmental role in the Mediterranean ecosystem.

In 1999, UNESCO proclaimed Ibiza as: "Ibiza, Biodiversity and Culture," a World Heritage City or Patrimony of Humanity, recognizing Ibiza as having special cultural or natural significance to the common heritage of humanity. The World Heritage Sites of Ibiza that are officially recognized by UNESCO include: the fields of Posidonia of Ses Salines Natural Park, the Phoenician settlement of sa Caleta, the fortifications of Ibiza City and the cemetery of Puig des Molins.

Posidonia is an endemic plant with leaves, stalks and fruit that forms dense prairies of Posidonia, or seagrass. The Posidonia is found in the Mediterranean Sea and is extremely important for the ecosystem because it supports a great diversity of marine life. In most parts of the Mediterranean the Posidonia is threatened, but in Ibiza, it remains well preserved. In this way, the Balearic Island provides a remarkable example of the interaction between marine and coastal ecosystems and greatly contributes to the biodiversity of marine life in the Mediterranean.

Additionally, Ibiza is acknowledged culturally because it preserves evidence of its long history. The island played an important role in the Mediterranean economy during the Phoenician-Carthaginian period as is exemplified by the archaeological site of Sa Caleta. Sa Caleta is a Phoenician settlement that was founded at the end of the 8th century BC and is the most important example of early Phoenician colonization. Sometime in the late 7th to the early 6th century BC, the settlers moved to a high hill dominating the bay where they founded the city of "Ibosim," the origin of the city of Ibiza.

Ibosim became the first city of the Balearic archipelago and the most important in the

Mediterranean region due to the maritime commerce of the Carthaginian Empire. In order to protect themselves from the Greeks and the Romans, the settlers fortified the acropolis with walls referred to traditionally as Dalt Vila and literally translated as "Upper Town". Throughout the history of construction earlier parts of the structure were incorporated into the fortification rather than destroyed, allowing the walls to preserve imprints of history that date back to early Phoenician settlements through to the Renaissance Age. In the 16th century the Dalt Vila, with Italian-Spanish engineering and military architecture mixed with Renaissance Age aesthetics, greatly influenced the creation of Spanish fortifications in the New World.

Approximately 500 m (1.640 ft) from the fortified walls of Ibiza's Dalt Vila is the archeological site of Puig des Molins. Puig des Molins is the best and most well conserved necropolis of Phoenician culture. Occupying over 50,000 m² (538,195 ft²), the cemetery contains over 3,000 Punic tombs. The most spectacular tombs found in Puig des Molins are called "hypogea," large subterranean chambers dug into rock which feature a well and an entrance door. Tourists can visit some of the hypogea tombs which have been equipped with lights and stairs.

Ibiza is much more than just beaches and sunshine. The Spanish island is full of historic sites dedicated to its vibrant past and incredible natural parks representing its grand biodiversity. To truly discover Ibiza, be sure to venture inland to the UNESCO World Heritage sites of sa Caleta, Dalt Vila, and Puig de Molins.

Why Travel to Ibiza?

Top Reasons to Travel to Ibiza

1. Nightlife

Surprise surprise, Ibiza's nightlife is one of the main draws to the island. With award-winning international dj's fighting to play there, the world's biggest clubs and most famous bars, if you're looking to party then Ibiza is the place to go. We've got the lowdown on the island's best bars and top Ibiza clubs so you make it to all the best fiestas. Visit Ibiza Nightlife.

2. Beaches

The 'white island' is world renowned for its long, beautiful coastline and endless choice of beaches. Whether you're looking for a lively spot to continue partying or an isolated cove to relax in, Ibiza has it all.

3. Weather

Ibiza has such a great climate it makes it a perfect holiday destination at any time of year. You can either choose to make the most of the boiling hot summer days and long balmy nights or escape for a bit of winter sun when the temperature is milder but the sun still shines.

4. Hippy Markets

Famous for its laid back boho vibe that has attracted hippies to Ibiza since the 70's, a trip to the island will not be complete without visiting one of its infamous hippy markets. You can pick up trinkets, jewellery, clothes and keepsakes to remind you of your trip.

5.Festivals

Summer parties aside, Ibiza has a whole lots of festivals which fill up the cultural calendar no end. Whether you want to catch a religious celebration or a traditional Balearic party, there is always something going on in Ibiza. Check out our Ibiza

Festivals calendar so you can plan your trip around one of the island's unforgettable fiestas

Ibiza is often referred to as the "white island" and "party capital of the world" a neat pair of monikers to describe the difference between day and night in this beautiful Spanish paradise. Ibiza is home to more than 60 beaches that attract visitors from all over the globe, and boasts some of the world's best nightclubs, which keep partiers entertained from sundown until dawn.

There are plenty of things to see and do in Ibiza, with a sunset boat cruise topping the list of relaxation. Beneath the waves, giant grouper and moray eels haunt the reefs and wrecks of the Mediterranean. Alternatively, visitors can explore the island's mystery and history on land at the Can Marca smugglers' caves, historic cemeteries, quaint villages, and pirate towers dotted about the island.

The beaches range from long popular stretches to secluded coves. However, Ibiza's natural attractions are not limited to just sand. The cliffs, mountains and nature reserves are known for their interesting variety of plant and animal species, including huge flocks of migrating flamingos that frequent Ses Salinas National Park every year towards summer's wane. These are balanced by manmade sights, including the World Heritage listed Dalt Villa, the charming walled old town.

Ibiza's popularity as a summer party spot means that it is imperative to book hotels and flights well in advance during the peak months of July and August when prices are up and availability is down. Many airlines run charters during high season, so savings are available to visitors willing to fly at unsociable hours on budget carriers. There are lots of options for accommodation, from budget hostels to 5-star luxury resorts and spas. Most are mid-range and focused either on families or young party people. Some visitors opt for a live-aboard sailing package for something a bit different. The food of the Balearic Islands is particularly appealing to lovers of Spanish cuisine and seafood, although pub grub, fast food and international favorites such as Indian and Italian are also readily available.

Ibiza has one airport, which welcomes about 95 percent of the island's visitors each year, although some come by ferry, yacht or cruise ship. Upon arrival, holidaymakers usually explore the island by public bus or rental car.

Ibiza Weather

Ibiza is one of Europe's hotspots for having fun in the sun and the weather is great year round. Whilst masses of sun worshippers and water babies hit the beaches in the scorching summer months, the warm winter days are equally as agreeable for those in search of sun without the burn, and beaches without the influx of sunbathers.

The summer season sees the hottest Ibiza weather and the lowest rainfall. May and October tend to sit very comfortably in the mid 20's (°C). Temperatures rocket between June and September, hitting the high 20's and 30's. The long sunny days and warm waters during the summer is the weather which attracts so many foreigners to the island who pass the time by living it up all night in the top Ibiza clubs and chilling out by day on the beaches. There is never a dull moment during Ibiza's buzzing summer months, however, it is also near impossible to find a solitary spot to unwind alone, so make sure you're ready for fun, sun and company.

Winter weather in Ibiza never comes close to the bitterly cold days and frosty nights that you and I may associate with winter. In actual fact, between the months of November and April, blue skies continue to abound and temperatures regularly hit 16°C and very rarely fall below 6 °C. However, after the madness that is the Ibizan summer, things tend to close up during the winter and it is the locals who enjoy the weather in Ibiza during this period. If you're looking for a relaxed break on empty beaches and a good dose of winter sun then this may be the perfect time to visit Ibiza.

Rainfall is minimal in Ibiza and the island is famed for having 300 days of sun each year. November-April sees more rain than the summer months, however, rain rarely falls for more than a couple of days at a time and is highly unlikely to tarnish your whole holiday.

Get a fix on the weather in Ibiza with our chart detailing average monthly highs and lows:

Month	Highs °C / °F	Lows °C / °F
January	13 / 55	4 / 39
February	14 / 57	5 / 41
March	16 / 60	8 / 46
April	17 / 62	9 / 48
May	20 / 68	13 / 55
June	24 / 75	16 / 60
July	27 / 80	19 / 66
August	28 / 82	19 / 66
September	26 / 79	18 / 64
October	21 / 70	13 / 55
November	17 / 62	8 / 46

| December | 14 / 57 | 7 / 44 |

Food & Drink

Ibiza food draws on the island's rich history and diverse culture to produce cuisine which is sure to suit all tastes, ages and budgets.

In popular coastal resorts you may find traditional British and German restaurants which serve up comforting home style classics to the hoards of tourists that arrive on the island in the summer months, many of whom are British and German. However, these summertime tourist pleasers are generally closed outside high season.

Tasty, traditional Spanish dishes are in abundance on a typical Ibizan menu. All the staple Spanish classics like Gazpacho (cold tomato soup) and Paella (saffron flavoured rice with vegetables/chicken/seafood) are widely available all over the island. Similarly, if you're partial to a bit of tapas, then you'll be pleased to hear you can indulge in Ibiza just as you would on the Spanish mainland. Tapas is a very social way of eating and traditionally forms the evening meal which takes place very late (not usually before 10pm). Families and groups of friends gather to 'picar' (literally 'nibble at') a selection of yummy little dishes. Seafood options come highly reccommended when in Ibiza, so make sure you include delectable delights like 'calamares' (fried squid) and 'gambas al ajillo' (garlic prawns) in your order.

Seafood in general is a must when sampling Ibiza food as it is all freshly caught without costing a bomb. Typical fish meals are served very simply, allowing you to truly relish the taste of the fish, which is normally just accompanied by potatoes and salad. You may also wish to try a local fish stew, known as 'Zarzuela', to get a taste of the best fish Ibiza has to offer.

More specific to the Balearic Island region are a few tasty treats that are not so common on the mainland. Balearic sausages, 'Sobresada' (blood sausage') and 'Butifarra' are the most famous ones and are definitely worth a try if you're not adverse to a bit of meat. You should also try Sofrit Pages, a truly hearty Balearic Island stew made from deliciously spiced lamb, pork, chicken, sausages and potatoes.

Ibiza food also contains some great treats for those of you with a sweet tooth. Most famous of all is the Ensaïmada de Mallorca. This sugary treat is widely available throughout the Balearic Islands and makes the perfect end to a perfect Ibizan meal. Ensaïmadas are made from a light pastry that can be filled with chocolate or cream, or just eaten plain with sugar dusted on top.

Another tasty pudding which is unique to the island of Ibiza is Flao. If you like cheesecake, you'll love this it is a mediterranean take on the American classic made with fresh cheese, mint, aniseed and honey. The taste is overall more herby than you may be used to, but it is definitely worth a try.

Almonds are another stock ingredient in any Ibiza dessert and you shouldn't leave without sampling a slice of scrumptious Gató d'Ametlla (almond cake) or a few scoops of almond ice cream on a hot day.

Got you tastebuds tingling? Check out our Ibiza drinks page and find something to wash all that delicious food down with!

Gastronomy

The islands of Ibiza and Formentera are called the "pinosas" because of their vast and luxuriant pine forests. These islands are very different from Majorca and Minorca, as tourists began to flock to them lured by the picturesque lifestyle that they offered and the excellent cuisine, based on seafood.

Fish

Fish and seafood are the most traditional foods in Ibiza. A very typical fish entree is ray with almonds, called burrida de ratjada and made with the most abundant nuts in the regions. Another popular recipe is the bullit, a rice with fish that is eaten backwards: first the boiled fish and then the rice. Try the anglerfish casserole, the bonito casserole with fennel and capers and the bull d'anfos, made with grouper's entrails and vegetables. As for the seafood, try the lobster from Ibiza, by itself or with squid. The guisat de marisc is another one of the delicious seafood dishes that we can have in the island of Ibiza. The salsa mosona is a very typical sauce in the islands, made by grinding almond, hazelnut and pine nut with hen liver and cinnamon. It is served with meat or fish stews, but it is really good with bread as an appetiser or as hors d'oeuvres.

Meat from Ibiza

As in the rest of the Balearic Islands, in Ibiza you will find the delicious coques, which are square pasties filled with meat, fish or chopped vegetables. Also popular is Catalan sausage from Ibiza and all the other sausages made with pork.

Other products

Formentera and Ibiza share a common culinary tradition. Fish is excellent and it is part of many island recipes, either guisat (in a stew with potatoes) or as the main ingredient in rice dishes. It is also excellent grilled. The cheese produced in Formentera is also of great quality, specially delicious with grapes and bread, especially if it is home-made bread. Flaó is the most typical dessert in this island.

Wines

With regards wine, the Balearic Islands currently have two Denominations of Origin: Binissalem and Pla i Llevant de Mallorca. Wine has been cultivated on the islands for thousands of years and the red wines tend to be more popular that the whites and rosés. The geographical denomination Vins de la Terra d'Eivissa protects the production of the popular wines made on the Island of Eivissa (Ibiza).

Ensaimadas and other delights

A meal is never complete if it is not finished off with one of the splendid local desserts. There are many to choose from: baked cottage cheese is the main milk pudding and another favourite is the "coca de albaricoques" (apricot cakes). But we mustn't forget the very traditional "ensaimadas" (spiral shaped pastries which are officially named Ensaïmadas de Mallorca) which are famous worldwide, or the small sponge cakes called "quartos", "rubiol", "crespell", "flaó" and "gató de almendra".

Liqueurs and ratafias

Traditional liqueurs are normally served with these delicious desserts or sometimes even as a drink before the meal, especially the Majorcan Palo liqueur (made from the carob fruit and with the geographic denomination Palo de Mallorca), the Herbes Mallorquines (made with herbs), Menorcan gin (Geographical denomination Gin de Menorca), the Herbes Eivissenques (also made with herbs and with the geographical denomination Herbes Eivissenques) and Frígola (mainly thyme).

Island Guide

Ibiza Town

Ibiza Town, or 'Eivissa', is likely to be your first stop when visiting the island. And what a memorable stop it will be! Ibiza's exciting and vivacious capital has got it all, and some more from the uber famous club scene that attracts armies of danceaholics each summer to the endearing Spanish traditions still alive and kicking in the old town. Need I mention the beaches?

Budding clubbers need no persuading that Ibiza town is an attractive and perfectly located city to make the most of Ibiza's nighttime sights, however, those of you in search of something a bit less hectic may be inclined to overlook the destination. Let me suggest you look again Ibiza town is home to some sleek hotels, attractive beaches, high quality restaurants and fascinating cultural landmarks.

Those of you that know what you're coming for and that involves a week or two of true exuberance strutting your stuff with fellow fashionistas, toned, tanned and raring to go, Ibiza town is also an obvious spot. In addition to killing the night before wiling away the days on party beaches, the new town offers affordable accommodation (as well as some rather VIP options like the Pacha hotel) and there is a cheap all night Disco Bus to ferry you to clubs outside the city.

But this very same destination can offer small town traditions, pretty architecture, majestic views, family friendly beaches and hidden coves for those of you that want to get away from it all. Ibiza town is also the site of many interesting cultural festivals which occur throughout the year check out our Festivals. It is also worth bearing in mind that Ibiza's fame for being a haven for hot-blooded hedonists can only be applied during the summer months (June-October) the rest of the year Ibiza town is a relatively relaxed spot to holiday in.

Never has one destination been so generous in catering for all tastes Ibiza town is definitely worth dedicating a good chunk of time to exploring, as whatever you hope to get out of Ibiza, you are sure to find a good part of it here.

Santa Eularia d'es Riu

Another of Ibiza's most popualar resorts is Santa Eularia d'es Riu (also known as Santa Eulalia d'es Riu). Located on the east coast of the island, Santa Eularia is a popular choice for families or those in search of a more chilled out break.

Located 15km from Ibiza Town, Santa Eularia is far enough away to deter the clubbers, but near enough to Ibiza airport to make it easily accesible for those heading there.

Regeneration of the town centre has led to a lot of development in Santa Eularia in recent years. The newly constructed beach front promenade has tidied up the town somewhat, however, Santa Eularia's popularity has led to mass construction of large luxury hotels and apartment blocks. Whilst the majority have been more nicely designed than the concrete blocks which line some beach resorts, the number of windows facing the beach succesfully destroys any hope of feeling secluded whilst you take a dip.

However, if its beach action you're after then in addition to the busy beach in the town itself, Santa

Eularia has lots of beautiful little sandy spots to discover if you fancy getting out the town.

Santa Eularia is also a region full of culture and history you can explore the charming old town or barter in Ibiza's infamous hippy markets. If you're not in search of all night clubs but aren't opposed to sipping a cocktail on a warm night after a good meal, Santa Eularia has some good options. Once again, the newly revamped beach front doesn't quite cut it and most of the eateries are more cheap and cheerful rather than sleek and classy. But if you dig a little deeper there are some great spots for quality dining (especially fish) and lively bars.

San Antonio de Portmany, Ibiza

San Antonio de Portmany is Ibiza's second largest resort and literally overflows with visitors between June and September every year.

For relaxation, solitude and authentic Spanish culture, please be warned that this is *not* the destination for you. However, if you're looking to party with an up-for-it crowd (almost entirely British), then San Antonio de Portmany 'San An' as it is known by those who love it will be like heaven.

Aesthetically, San Antonio de Portmany lacks the charm of Ibiza Town, as many of the buildings are new high rise hotel blocks filled with package deal punters. Nonetheless, the town has seen huge investments in recent years as the council has attempted to regenerate the urban centre and make it more attractive and stylish. The main promenade has been tidied up and lined with palm trees, an artificial beach has been created right in the centre of the town and tons of trendy new bars have opened in an attempt to inject some of that Ibiza Town chic into San An's cheap and tacky façade.

Nonetheless, San Antonio de Portmany is getting better and if you want a well located destination (just a 20 minute bus ride from Ibiza Town), with nice beaches nearby, crazy nightlife and infamous sunsets then San An could be just the place for you. If you decide to visit San Antonio de Portmany just outside of high season (May or October) you will find a more laid back vibe and a less exaggerated foreign invasion, however, in the winter months there is very little open in this part of Ibiza.

Portinatx, Ibiza

Totally different from Ibiza's other main resorts, Portinatx is the perfect place to head if you want to avoid the troops of clubbers and make the most of the 'other Ibiza' idyllic vistas and hidden beaches without the thud of a bassline forming the soundtrack.

Whether you're all clubbed out, looking for a romantic retreat or an ideal destination for a family holiday Portinatx is Ibiza's prime spot. Being a popular resort it has most amenities, but developers have taken care not to ruin the area with lots of unsightly highrises. Whilst Portinatx, tends to be frequented by a less party-crazed crowd, that is not to say it is empty especially between June and September when it is constantly alive with the buzz of holidaymakers.

Portinatx, Ibiza is perfectly positioned on the northernmost point of the island to facilitate your exploration of the northern coastline. There are dozens of perfect little bays to be discovered, good restaurants to enjoy and sporting opportunities to be had in this beautiful part of Ibiza..

Places to Visit

biza is packed full with places to visit, so make sure you get up in time to enjoy the day as well as the long summer nights on this paradise island. Whether you want to rave it up on a happening beach or escape it all in you own little cove, we've got the lowdown on places to visit in Ibiza. And if you've done the beaches to death there are some other interesting day trips to make your trip to Ibiza even more memorable...

Ibiza Beaches

Many people who choose to holiday in Ibiza have one principal objective to enjoy the island's plethora of sun-drenched beaches. The beauty of Ibiza's coastline is that there are beaches to suit all tastes. Whether you want an isolated cove to bask in the sun, to continue partying from the night before, or seek out a family friendly place, there will be an Ibiza beach to suit your needs you just need to know where to look for it.

Whilst many of Ibiza's biggest resorts are packed during the summer months with clubbers and families alike all fighting for a place to set up camp, there are endless places to escape to if you're looking for a bit of peace and quiet or are in search of a more unique beach bar experience. Check out our Ibiza beach guide and get the lowdown on the best places for fun and total relaxation.

Best Ibiza Beaches: Relaxing

If you're looking for a secluded sandy spot or an uncommercialised bit of coastline you need to get out of the big resorts in Ibiza. However, that does not mean to say that they are necessarily miles away from where you might be staying in fact, nothing is too far away in Ibiza. With a hire car or a local bus service, you can get away from the masses in half an hour. We've got the lowdown on the best Ibiza beaches for taking the kids or truly chilling out, so sit back, have a read, and prepare to relax...

Talamanca

Just a tiny bit further up the coast from Ibiza town, this is a perfectly located beach if you want to escape the clubbers and the bars which are commonplace on most of the other beaches in the area. Talamanca is popular with families and is not a secret getaway, however, it is a safe, accesible, sandy option for some relaxed beach action.

Cala Llenya

This little cove is a favourite with locals and is located just up from the Santa Eularia resort. There is a mixture of sand and rocks at this untouched and attractive spot. Not so highly recommended for young children, but it's perfect for couples or groups of friends looking for a bit of peace and quiet.

Cala Mastella

Another chilled out beach within easy striking distance from Santa Eularia, Cala Mastella is an idyllic spot especially for those who like snorkelling. Amenitites are few and far between here, so bring your own lunch! There is an infamous fish restaurant in the cove (make sure you reserve in person the day before you plan to eat there).

Cala Pada

A cute, sandy beach just a stone's throw from Santa Eularia, Cala Pada is recommended for those in search of a totally untouched little gem of a beach.Niu Blau

This great sandy beach is a beautiful, tranquil place to spend the days and is easily accesible from

Santa Eularia, however, after the sun goes down it often springs into action with beach parties. This reputation means it tends to attract a younger crowd.

Cala Moli

If you're based at San Antonio de Portmany and want to escape the noise of the city, this is a perfect choice. You need a car to get here and it's a bit tricky to find so is only recommended to those who are confident on the roads. However, this means that is never gets too packed which is what keeps it so special.

Cala Salada

This is another popular choice with clubbed out clubbers and families alike. The secret is out and this cove does get pretty full during the summer months so it isn't an isolated option, nonetheless, it has a nice chilled out vibe and feels very safe.

Cala Salada is just north of San Antonio de Portmany and whilst the main beach is generally busy, the northern cove is a lot quieter.

Benirrás

This incredible beach manages to enchant all types of people. It doesn't get too busy during the day when families and friends come to enjoy the beautiful surroundings and nice water. At sunset it is famous for attracting hippies who bang on their bongos into the night, attracting those who want to wile away their evening in an extremely relaxed fashion. Benirrás is most easily accesible from San Miguel inland and Portinatx along the coast.

Cala Xuclar

Located a tiny way west from Portinatx, Cala Xuclar is undoubtedly one of the best Ibiza beaches for enjoying some beautiful scenery without too much company. The beach tends to attract locals but it is suitable for everyone, just be warned there are not many facilities here so come prepared!

Cala Xarraca

Right next to Xuclar you will find another perfect little cove to explore Cala Xarraca makes a great getaway from Portinatx. There are more pebbles than sand, but there is some great snorkelling to be had here and a lovely day out for everyone.

Top Ibiza Beaches: Parties

If you're not worn out by the crazy Ibiza nightlife you may be in search of a place to party by day. The beaches are most definitely where it's at in Ibiza and while they are often a lot quieter during the winter, if you're there for the madness of an Ibizan summer you'll have a huge choice of pumping beachside parties to enjoy in the sun. We've done a reccy to find you the top Ibiza beaches for partying so that you can be sure to end up where the music is blaring and everyone is there to have a good time.

Platja d'en Bossa

Ibiza's most famous party beach takes traditional beach bars to a new level. Home to the infamous Space and Bora Bora bar, Platja d'en Bossa is the place for danceaholics. We're talking serious, hardcore partying 24 hours a day. Not for the fainthearted!

Figueretes

Ibiza Town's most conveniently located beach is not the world's prettiest beach but is a popular spot with tons of beach bars and a constant buzz all summer long.

Salines

Touted as the top Ibiza beach, Ses Salines is an attractive place to spend the day with clean water and perfect white sand. It has also become *the* place to be seen on the island and is definitely worth a little excursion south of Ibiza Town. The partying is not as manic as on Platja d'en Bossa, making it the perfect spot to perfect your tan, sip a cocktail and mingle with the beautiful people whilst the DJ pumps out laid back tunes.

Playa d'es Cavallet

Very popular with gay visitors, this rugged and wild looking sandy beach is home to some funky beach bars and a lot of nudity. If you're coming from Ibiza Town, Playa d'es Cavallet is just before the turn off for Ses Salines.

San Antonio Beach

The government's plan to make San Antonio de Portmany more beautiful mainly centred around the creation of a 'perfect' beach right in the centre of the town. The result is white sand, palm trees and a lot of people. Definitely a convenient stop if you're staying in San An, the beach is always lively and is lined with touristy bars and restaurants, however, if you're looking for a more classy affair, we'd reccommend you get out the city.

Cala Conta

These beaches just west of San Antonio de Portmany come highly recommended. The motto here is not just party, party, party and many families come to enjoy the nice surroundings. However, the beach is home to some cool beach bars and attracts a trendy, fun loving crowd.

Santa Eularia Beach

As with many of the beaches located in the cities, Santa Eularia beach is a bit of an eyesore, none the less, there are plenty of bars, great watersports and lots of people enjoying sun, sea and fun together.

Niu Blau

Also recommended in our best Ibiza beaches for chilling, Niu Blau strikes the perfec balance. The stunning cove embodies what beaches are all about really sand, clean water and great sunsets. It is truly relaxed during the day, but at night often hosts some amazing beach parties perfect if you fancy a change from the clubs. Niu Blau is just a stone's throw (north) from Santa Eularia.

Cala Llonga

One of the hotspots on any clubber's agenda Cala Llonga is a thriving beach resort minus the slabs of concrete dropped on the likes of San Antonio, making it a prettier place to spend the day. Located just south from Santa Eularia, Cala Llonga is packed with holidaymakers in the summer and has a busy, buzzing vibe and lots of amenities.

Playa Porto, S'arenal Gros, S'arenal Petit

These are the most accesible bays if you are in Portinatx. For a beach resort, they are really pretty and the hotels which surround them have gone some way to not ruin the vistas. In the summer months these beaches are heaving with people a less party crazed crowd than the island's other resorts, but a fun loving atmosphere all the same.

Benirrás

Just a stone's throw from Portinatx, Cala Benirrás is up there with Ses Salines in Ibiza's top beaches. This is not for hardcore partying but more for those of you that enjoy watching the sunset whilst dancing to the rhythmic patter of bongos. By day this beach is a relaxed, family friendly spot but at sunset the hippies arrive to spread the love (and the beer). A truly perfect way to spend an evening if you want a breather from the mayhem of Ibiza's clubs

Cueva de Can Marça, Ibiza

If you're looking for a different kind of Ibiza day trip then why not get away from the beaches and bars and visit the Cueva de Can Marça? A truly fascinating outing for all ages just a little way west from Ibiza's northern resort of Portinatx.

Before entering the caves you can take in the most breathtaking views over the coast at Puerto de San Miguel. The Cuevas de Can Marça are made up of lots of adjoining underground caves which were once used by smugglers to hide their goods. The eery ambience is made even more spectacular with a hi-tech light and music show, perfectly timed with the guided tour.

Once down in the caves there are some unforgettable geological rock formations dating back 100,000 years. You can see where water once used to run and admire the enormous 30 foot waterfall which plunges down to the depths of the caverns, conjuring up what life used to be like down in the Cuevas de Can Marça.

You can visit the caves throughout the year:-
Summer Opening Hours: 10.30am-7.30pm
Winter opening Hours: 11am-5pm

Ibiza Theme & Water Parks

A holiday in the sun is not complete without a trip to a waterpark and Ibiza has plenty of choice. Kids and adults alike can spend a day screeching with delight as they shoot down slides and splash about in pools. It's a great idea for families or groups of friends who fancy a change from the beach.

Ibiza has two water parks, both very close to Ibiza town but easy to get to from any part of the island. Check out our reviews to decide which is best for your needs:

Aguamar Water Park, Ibiza

The island's biggest and baddest waterpark is undoubtedly Aguamar. Situated in Playa d'en Bossa, Aguamar is a quick 15 minute trip from Ibiza Town and buses leave regularly, if you don't have a car. Located just behind Ibiza's legendary Space nightclub, Aguamar is a popular choice for adults and kids. There is such a big variety of slides to keep all ages entertained all day long. You can bring a picnic or make use of the massive choice of restaurants and cafés in the park. This is definitely the best choice for clubbers who fancy a break from dancing or families who want a bit more action.

Aguamar Water Park
Playa d'en Bossa, Ibiza
Tel: (0034) 971 300 671

Open between mid June and October

Entrance fees vary (family, children, concession...)

Agualandia Water Park, Ibiza

Agualandia comes more highly recommended for families with small children as the slides are smaller and less varied. There is still plenty of space for onlooking parents to picnic, sunbathe or grab a bite to eat. Agualandia is in Talamanca, just north of Ibiza town and makes a nice trip from Talamanca's family friendly beach.

Agualandia Water Park

Talamanca, Ibiza

Tel: (0034) 971 190 661

Open between June and October

Entrance fees vary

Culture & the Arts

Museums in Ibiza, Spain

Whilst most people don't come to Ibiza for its museums, if you fancy a break from sunning yourself then the island has a good handful of interesting exhibitions, galleries and archeological sites to keep you amused. Most are found in Ibiza Town but there are a splattering in other parts of the island.

Museu Archeològic

Ibiza's intereting archeological museum is the perfect place to head if you're interested in finding out about the island's diverse history. The museum contains artefacts and information about Ibiza from prehistoric times through Phoenician, Punic, Roman and Islamic eras.

Address: Plaza de la Catedral 3, Ibiza Town
Tel: (0034) 971 301 231
Opening Hours (Closed Mondays)
AprilSeptember: Tues-Sat: 10am-2pm/ 5pm-8pm,

Sun: 10am-2pm

October-March: Tues-Sat: 10am-1pm/ 4pm-6pm, Sun: 10am-2pm

Museu d'Art Contemporani

The only contemporary art museum on the island, this is definitely worth a look if you enjoy perusing modern art. The museum features frequently changing paintings and sculpture by international artists.

Address: Ronda de Narcis Puget

Tel: (0034) 971 302 723

Opening Hours (Closed Mondays)

April-September: Tues-Fri 10am-1.30pm/ 5pm-8pm. Weekends: 10am-1.30pm

October-March: Tues-Sun 10am-1.30pm

Necròpolis del Puig des Molins

This Phoenician-Punic burial ground is of great importance to archeologists and historians studying the Phoenician occupation of the west mediterranean. The site contains a huge number of tombs and an intricate network of underground caverns which link them together. Puig des Molins was named a UNESCO World heritage site in 1999, along with the historic centre of Ibiza town, D'Alt Vila.

Address: Vía Romana 31, **Ibiza Town**

Tel: (0034) 971 301 771

Opening Hours (Closed Mondays)

April-September: Tues-Sat 10am-2pm/5pm-8pm, Sun: 10am-2pm

October-March: Tues-Sat 10am-2pm/6pm-8pm, Sun 10am-2pm

Museu Etnològic

This Santa Eularia based ethnological museum is packed with information relating to the cultural development of Ibiza and Formentera. You can see a wide range of artefacts from traditional dress to the rise of the farming industry in this part of the Balearics.

Address: Can Ros, Puig de Misa, Santa Eularia
Opening Hours (Closed Sundays)
Mondays: 4pm-6pm
Tuesdays-Saturdays: 10am-1pm/ 4pm-6pm

Aquarium Cap Blanc

Whilst not strictly speaking a 'museum', this lovely aquarium makes a great day out for anyone in the San Antonio vicinity. It is so special as it is built into a natural underground cave. You can see a whole host of typical Balearic Island marine life here.

Address: Cova de ses Llegostes, Carretera de Cala Gració, San Antonio de Portmany.

Ibiza Dance Music

What we have already seen throughout this guide is that there is much, much more to Ibiza than just clubs and clubbers. Nonetheless, the little island's rise to fame as a global dance capital cannot be ignored, nor can the fact that the evolution of important contemporary musical genres occured within its bars and clubs. Ibiza dance music is an eclectic and exciting topic which attracts and inspires the world's best dj's and music fanatics year in and year out. We take a look at Ibiza's journey to becoming the world's most coveted clubbing destination and find out what it is that makes Ibiza such a special place to party...

It all began in the 1960's when 'the hippies' arrived on the island. Still a prominent feature today, surviving hippies in Ibiza cash in with their markets (see Ibiza shopping for details) and thrill tourists by banging their bongos on beaches at sunset. Originally these wanderers with long hair hailed from the U.S and brought with them musical styles that hadn't yet reached Spain. Francisco Franco was in power until 1975 and attempted to prohibit the importation of foreign bands. Nonetheless, Ibiza blossomed as an innovative home for music and the word began to spread. Trendsetters and music buffs headed to Ibiza to host enormous parties on farms in the countryside, which gave rise to a huge amount of musical productivity and freedom.

Ibiza's fate was really sealed when Pacha Ibiza opened in 1973. Finally, the partiers had a proper place to do their thing. By the time Franco's dictatorship ended the word was out. The island's first superclub attracted budding acts from all over the world and its insane popularity gave rise to more clubs, namely Amnesia and Es Paradis. All of these clubs continue going strong today, see top

Ibiza clubs for the scoop on these legendary Ibiza hotspots and more.

Free from Franco's laws, the end of the 70's and right into the 80's Ibiza became a playground for musical experimentation. Its global reputation meant that Ibiza was visited by people from all over the world, each bringing with them the trends from their own hometowns. Things weren't necessarily new in Ibiza, what was exciting was the emergence of a space where musical styles from far flung parts of the world were put in close contact with each other, allowing ideas to spread and develop.

During the 1990's Ibiza became inextricably linked to the development of the electronic dance revolution. Rave culture, drugs and 24 hour parties backed by the soundtrack of synthesised beats that just have to be danced to made clubbers flock to Ibiza. Dance music cannot be polarised, but rather it describes a plethora of categories and sub-categories that have continued to gain popularity over the last 3 decades. In particular, House music has gone from strength to strength and Ibiza has played a huge role in making it accesible to more people.

What Ibiza has come to represent is an area where music can evolve. Many people try to label it as the birth place of certain genres, but this is a controversial idea to push. In my opinion, Ibiza has become a liberal space within which different styles can fuse and develop especially dance music and all its sub-genres. As well as becoming the crème de la crème for any famous DJ to play at, Ibiza is an eclectic platform with the power to make or break the career of any new DJ.

What many people have always loved about Ibiza is that such a huge variety of music can be heard there and this is no less true today than it was forty years ago. Ibiza has become such a popular destination that clubs dedicate rooms to totally different musical styles from latin and garage to r'n'b and hip hop. It has even been said that 2008 will see the likes of brit indie rock band the Kaiser Chiefs performing in Ibiza.

Whilst noone can predict the future of Ibiza dance music, we can be sure that it will continue to develop, evolve and thrive between the bars and clubs of this very special island.

Theatre & Concert Venues in Ibiza

It has to be said that Ibiza is most certainly hotter on clubs than theatres and concert venues. Nonetheless, if you are looking for a little dose of live music there are a few places worth checking out. If it's serious theatre or opera you're after, then you'll need to travel to Mallorca (which has endless theatres) or Menorca which has a very renowned theatre with a full programme of events. See the following list for the most popular Balearic island and Ibiza theatre and concert halls.

Teatro Pereira

Not strictly speaking a theatre, this cool bar in Ibiza Town makes for the perfect hangout if you want to get off the Ibiza club circuit. There are frequently live music gigs so it's worth ringing in advance to see what's on while you're in town.

Address: Carrer del Comte de Rosselló 3, Ibiza Town
Tel: (0034) 971 1914

Guaranà

The top spot in Santa Eularia if you want to catch a live show. At this trendy locale you can catch blues and jazz bands..
Address: Passeig Marítím, Santa Eularia

Auditorium de Palma de Mallorca
If you want to see some traditional theatre in the Balearics you're gonna have to head to Mallorca. This beautiful theatre-cum-conference auditorium has year round arts events.
Address: Paseo Maritimo 18, Palma de Mallorca
Tel: (0034) 971 734 735

Iguana Teatre
Another hotspot for theatre in Palma de Mallorca is the Iguana theatre.
Address: Capitán Ramonell Boix 90, Palma de Mallorca
Tel: (0034) 971 246 200

Teatre Mao

Alternatively, if you're planning on visiting Menorca, there is a great little theatre with a variety of performances in the island's capital city.

Address: Carretera Deía 40, Mao, Menorca

Tel: (0034) 971 355 603

Ibiza Holidays and Festivals

A largely Catholic nation like Spain, many Ibiza holidays and events revolve around the religious calendar. Easter Holy Week is a major occasion with elaborate processions being common across the Balearic Islands on Good Friday. It is an interesting quirk that Spain's major gift giving day is not on December 25, as in most Christian countries, but on January 6 when the Three Kings arrived bearing presents.

In Ibiza, it is possible to attend first order theatrical productions, to poetry recitals and countless exhibitions and displays that take place in all seasons, in the different museums or in the art rooms inhabiting the different towns of the island. The annual Festival of Jazz, held in the capital of the Pitiüses, is the personification of this cultural and leisure diversification. A musical event which has gradually become more prestigious and promotes the young musicians of this genre in the Mediterranean. On the other hand, its traditional fiestas provide a unique range of celebrations to help you really get to know the local culture.

Sant Antoni de Portmany patron saint

Sant Antoni Abad is possibly one of the most celebrated saints in the towns of the Illes Balears. However, the 17th January is a particularly special day for Sant Antoni de Portmany, in Eivissa. When this day arrives, the town is decked out to pay tribute to its patron saint, the good Sant Antoni. The Passeig de Ses

Fonts is where a large part of the activities which are organised for this day take place. This lovely promenade makes its way between gardens and fountains, skirting the large, calm bay of Sant Antoni de Portmany, on the eastern coast of Eivissa. The Romans called this place Portus Magnus (Big Port), from which the present name apparently is derived. Perhaps alluding to this splendour, there is a monument at the entrance of the bay which commemorates Christopher Columbus; a stone egg with a caravel inside. The fiestas begin a few days before the commemoration of the saint, with different activities; competitions, concerts and other events provide enjoyment for everyone.

Animal blessing and parade of Moors and Christians

On the 17th January, a mass is held in the morning in honour of the saint, followed by a procession and the traditional blessing of the animals. Many of the people of Sant Antoni also dress up as Moors and Christians on this day and take part in an impressive parade which arouses admiration in those watching. The baile payés (country dance), to the rhythm of typical Ibizan instruments such as the flute, and lively street parties bring a touch of music to the festival. It is well worth visiting this town, which still conserves its character as a 'caserío pescador' (fishing village), as it was called at the turn of the 20th Century. Its streets are steep and narrow, with beautiful buildings offering a variety of restaurants, shops and other businesses. It also retains a certain hippie air, suggesting that the pace of life is somewhat different here and full of colour. This is also an excellent place for enjoying sunsets from the coast, with the islet of Conillera enclosing the bay not very far away.

Festes de la Terra

Eivissa town turns into a vibrant centre of fun and commemorative events during the first eight days of August. This is the Festes de la Terra (Festival of the Earth), held in honour of the patron saints, Mary ?ad nives? and Saint Cyriacus, which celebrates the Catalan conquest of Ibiza on the 8th of August 1235. Fun is guaranteed by the many activities on offer throughout this week of festivities: competitions, exhibitions, street music, performances in squares... as well as traditional religious events such as those that take place on the 5th of August, the day of the Virgin, and in the Sant Ciriac festival on the 8th. The latter date commemorates the conquest of Ibiza by the Catalan troops in 1235, one of the most significant and popularly acclaimed celebrations. In the morning a mass is sung in honour of the saint . After that, a street procession accompanies the parishioners who file by with their flags. Not all of them have these banners and the oldest of them, made over two hundred years ago belongs to the Sant Llorenç parish. Some of these flags have featured in curious anecdotes; the emblem of Sant Jordi for example, which they had to bury in order to hide it during the Civil War.

Un alto en la capilla de Sant Ciriac

The Sant Ciriac chapel, a small temple from the 18th Century is an essential stop-off. Below the saint there is an unusual, crude looking arch wherein lies a tale. Legend has it that the arch formed part of the passageway through which the Christians entered in 1235, led by the embittered brother of the Muslim sheikh of the time. Today the custom is to throw coins inside for luck. The parade ends up at the monument to Guillem de Montgrí, with an offering of flowers and group dances, ball pagès (country dancing). On this same day, as dusk begins to fall, the villagers go up to Puig des Molins to take their berenada (a light tea) of pies, sandwiches and other home-made dishes. Live street bands, musical performances, and a spectacular castle of fireworks add the final touch to these festivities.

Festa del Vi Pagès

The Festa del Vi Payés is a tribute to Bacchus, the god of wine. But not only is good wine drunk on this day; sobrasadas and butifarras from the recent pig slaughter are grilled outdoors over wood fires to accompany these exquisite wines. On the initiative of the small-scale wine producers of this village, the Festa del Vi Payés (Country Wine Festival) emerged as an attraction, since the sale of bottled wine had considerably reduced the demand for the typical local wines. Over the years, this festival has become a social event which brings together more than five thousand people, in a village with a population numbering less than 400. Of the four brands of wines registered in Ibiza, three are from Sant Mateu, two of them with the Denominació d?Origen Ibiza (Ibiza Guarantee of Origin). This village, which belongs to the municipal district of Sant Antoni de Portmany, nestles among the mountains and has good dry land, composed of a type of very strong clay. Since time immemorial the country folk have cultivated their vines producing wine on a small scale.

Wine and products of the pig slaughter

oday the number of small-scale wine producers has increased to twenty five, and there are also two bodegas or wineries in operation. They all ensure that the wine flows freely during this festival, with each of them donating a demijohn of wine which, altogether, comes to about 800 litres. The food side is also important. So two weeks earlier, the pig slaughter takes place, one of the most deeply-rooted popular customs in the Illes Balears, and they prepare sobrasadas (spicy Mallorcan sausages) and butifarras (pork sausages) which, grilled over wood fires, will accompany the wine during this festival. Merienda or supper begins at six o?clock in the evening in the municipal sports centre of the village. Already alight at this hour are ingenious barbecues set up over old bathtubs, a very efficient system for keeping the fire going. All around are stalls where typical Ibizan products can be bought and stands where they make fresh buñuelos (fritter doughnuts) on the spot. Music and fun accompany the fiesta which lasts until midnight, while the wine helps one to forget the incipient cold of winter.

Feast of the Epiphany

Celebrations begin on the evening of January 5, where the costumed Three Kings arrived in the port of Ibiza by ship to join an elaborate procession of floats. The parade moves through town, stopping to bless Baby Jesus at the church before congregating in the square where the names of children receiving gifts are read by the Magi. The next day is the Feast of the Epiphany, which commemorates the arrival of the three kings in Bethlehem. The children wake to find Los Reyes Magos (the kings) have left presents if they have been good or coal (chocolate shaped like coal) if they have been bad.

Carnaval

Ibiza's Carnaval is a mardi gras style celebration that usually takes place in February, 40 days before Easter. Marking the last party before the Catholic fast of Lent, the week-long festival features fancy costumes, food, cart racing from the hill of old town to Vara de Rey, concerts in the Plaza del Parque, a parade, a children's fiesta, live music, barbeques, street stalls, dancing, and general merriment. Most of the action is around central park and the harbor.

Easter

Semana Santa, or Easter, the Christian crucifixion and resurrection of Jesus Christ, is the major religious occasion in Ibiza in early April. Good Friday processions are one of the main events where hundreds of hooded followers from various "brotherhoods" carry sacred statues of saints around town. The Santa Eulalia parade begins in the market at 10:00 a.m. and includes a reenactment of the Stations of the Cross. The processional ends at the church high on the hill at the town's entrance. There is a midday concert in the square, and then the procession continues to the Chapel of Lourdes in the town center at 8:00 p.m.

Ibiza International film Festival

The Ibiza International Film Festival (IFF) has been hosted every May since 2007, and features movie screenings leading up to an extravagant awards ceremony. "The independent spirit" slogan reflects the event's premise to celebrate films in 17 categories, such as best picture and script. The prize is a Falcó d'Or, a statuette of the cliff-nesting Eleonora Falcon of Ibiza, which also gives a nod to the movie, the *Maltese Falcon*.

First Sunday in May

The first Sunday in May sees the town of Santa Eulalia shut down for a fiesta to commemorate the miraculous 14th century collapse of a church roof after everyone had vacated. The event is celebrated with a massive parade of decorated horse-drawn carriages, riders and the municipal band. In modern times, the event has also attracted antique car clubs, agricultural equipment, races, and food.

Dia del Carmen

Virgin del Carmen, the patron saint of the fisherman, has her day on July 16 every year, which is a public holiday in the fishing towns of Ibiza and San Antonio. Celebrations include parades such as the colorful water procession through Ibiza town, and feature flower-filled boats that congregate around the harbor. The seaside town of Portinatx has one of the more notable fiestas with boats laying wreaths at sea. There are also concerts, feasting, street stalls, and beach parties.

Christmas

Christmas is an important religious celebration in Ibiza, where popular Christmas markets and fairs lead up to Christmas Eve. Vara del Rey Plaza is the center for civic celebrations, decked out as a winter wonderland with decorated stalls and a massive tree. Ibiza's Christmas lights are usually turned on by December 1, and intricate nativity scenes start to appear halfway through the month. Christmas Eve, or Nochebuena (Goodnight), is characterized by family get togethers for drinks and food followed by midnight mass. Many restaurants offer special set menus on Christmas day, which need to be booked in advance.

Leisure Activities

Visitors can not only enjoy magnificent beaches in the Balearic Islands, but also a wide range of leisure centres, nature parks that showcase fauna and waterfowl, impressive natural caves, manor homes, world-famous archaeological remains and more. An array of cultural and entertainment activities to suit the most varied tastes. A myriad of alternatives also exist for nightlife.

Evissa Ibiza

The city of Eivissa offers to its visitors a varied supply of leisure. The districts of the Port, La Marina and Playa d'en Bossa concentrate the nocturnal diversion of the city.

The native night of Eivissa is famous throughout the world: Discos, bars, pubs, restaurants invade the streets of the island and illuminate with their lights the native night of Eivissa. The supply is so varied that it would not be right to mention concrete places, being able to enjoy widely the multiple atmospheres that the city presents.

For those who prefer to enjoy the day, Eivissa also offers a varied supply to them: sport facilities where to practice their favorite sport, beaches qualified for the practice of marine sports or to dive and discover the beautiful marine bottoms of the island, and other centers where, for example, enjoy a horse ride by the inner Eivissa.

The supply is complemented with other spaces and artisan activities of leisure such as cinemas, concerts, rooms of game, markets where buying becomes a colorful experience, etc.

Puig des Molins

The archaeological site of the Puig des Molins situated at the foot of the mountain of same name, next to the "Museu Arqueològic del Puig des Molins" (at the moment closed due to renovations), was the cemetery of Eivissa since the foundation of the city by Occidental Phoenicians at the end of the VII century BC. The initial necropolis experimented an important development in the Punic era, to be precise from the VI century BC to the end of the I century AC, reaching 50.000

square metres of occupied area. The cemetery was still used in the Roman era from the I to the V century AC and also later in the VI and VII centuries AC.

The site is the biggest and best conserved necropolis of the Phoenician-Punic culture with over 3.000 Punic tombs with chamber and access well called hypogeums, although only 340 are visible from outside. Visitors to the site can enter a group of hypogeum equipped with lights and stairs.

In 1977 the necropolis of the Puig des Molins was declared a Property of Cultural Interest and in 1999, together with the fortified area of Dalt Vila, the Phoenician settlement of sa Caleta and the prairies of Posidonia of the Natural Park of ses Salines, was declared World Heritage by Unesco.

Visiting times:

Summer (from March 16 to October 15): Tuesdays to Saturdays from 10 a.m. to 2 p.m. and 6 to 8 p.m. Sundays from 10 a.m. to 2 p.m. Mondays and festivities closed.

Winter (from October 16 to March 15): Tuesdays to Saturdays from 9 a.m. to 3 p.m. Sundays from 10 a.m. to 2 p.m. Mondays and festivities closed. Free entrance.

San Antonio

The second largest town on the island, San Antonio was originally called Portus Magnus by the Romans. Its full title is Sant Antoni de Portmany or San Antonio Abad (Castilliano & Catalan respectively).

The older part of the town extends from the 16th Century church down to the port area, as this was originally a fishing village. This is the area known nowadays as the West End and fishermen are scarce. The port, being a natural harbour in a strategic position in the middle of the Mediterranean, played an important role in the island's history for many centuries as different civilisations invaded the island.

Unfortunately, still recovering from a sleezy reputation, courtesy of bad press in all forms of media, this used to be the main tourism centre of the island back in the early days. This was because the other towns of the island encouraged people to cover all exposed flesh, even in the height of summer, and discouraged dancing other than on fiesta days meaning complex folk dancing only!

San Antonio was then more permissive and attracted tourists from mainland Europe to the island, to the extent that it became the San Tropez of the Balearics if not the southern Mediterranean. In those halcyon days the West End was the best place on the island to find the finest restaurants and rub shoulders with the often aristocratic yacht owners whose craft were moored in the beautiful, unspoilt bay.

These days, during the main clubbing season of July & August, it heaves with young people enjoying their first holidays without their parents learning about adolescence, drinking, music, dancing and the opposite sex etc. The two months before and after these two are dominated by families, with big smiles on their faces, enjoying the incredible range of entertainment options available and the beautiful nearby beaches, just a short ferry ride away.

Santa Eularia

The island's third largest town, but allegedly the richest town in all of Spain per capita, Santa Eulalia sits 15km north of Ibiza town on the eastern coast of the island. It dominates the mouth of the only river in the entire Balearic Island group and for this reason has always been of enormous strategic importance to the island. The walk along the river is lovely in itself, despite the fact that it has dried up over the years as the water table on the island has fallen, it now runs for barely half a kilometre to the old Roman bridge that used to serve the town, but the ducks that live beneath the bridge are an unusual sight.

Santa Eulalia has a larger indiginous population than San Antonio, the second largest town, and for this reason changes its character little in or out of season. Perhaps the locals have sussed the succession of beautiful beaches from Agua Blanca in the north all the way down to Ibiza town and realised that this is the perfect base? Unfortunately though, over recent years the pace of development around the fringes of the town have doubled its size so perhaps the locals talk too much.

At the top of the hill as you enter the town from Ibiza sits the most imposing church you are ever likely to see. The most complete example of the characteristic local architecture to be found on the island, apart from the fortress of Ibiza old town itself. Built in the 16th Century to replace one previously destroyed by the Turks, it is a complex of annexes topped with domes to either side of the nave, and hilltop shade from which the views over the island are magnificent. At night the hill with the church at its crest are floodlit making the arrival over the river bridge into Santa Eulalia from Ibiza a special experience.

Turning right at any point upon entering the town one arrives at the long promenade which runs the entire length of the two beaches between the river's mouth and the marina. This is lined with mature trees and divided by a big fountain at its centre. It is also lined with a huge selection of cafe's and restaurants along its length. In addition within the town, set back from the beach a couple of hundred meters, is the famous 'Restaurant Street' reinforcing the town's reputation for providing the widest range of quality, gastronomic options available on the island.

A cosmopolitan town with a relatively small 'seasonal' population, it changes little from one season to the other, unlike many other resorts on the island.

Las Dalias and Punta Arabi

In San Carlos in the North-East, set in the grounds of a restaurant, this weekly market continues in Saturdays throughout the year. Many consider it to be a more original and traditional alternative to the larger Wednesday market at Es Caná. Wonderful selection of handmade clothes and jewellery, you can be sure to find that little something for everyone. Open until late in summer, 'til 18.00 in winter, every Saturday.

A visit to the famous Hippy Market on the grounds of the holiday club Punta Arabí in Es Cana, near Santa Eulalia, held every Wednesday (from may to october) from 10.00 19.00 hrs., is a must. At the market you have an enormous variety to choose from: the most exotic batik wraps and clothing to tailor-made leather mocassins and an tantalising variety of east-asian silver jewellry and trinkets. If you look around you can still find some of the original hippies, although most of them have grey hair by now! Like a time-warp back to the 1970s. Every Wednesday.

Puerto de San Miguel

A quiet little hamlet near to the inhospitable northern coast of Ibiza, which roughly translated means "the gateway to the unspoilt coast of the north". A beautiful old 18th Century church surrounded by a few houses forms the obvious 'village', but in years gone by this was the heart of local civilisation when Sunday came around and the outlying population met to congregate and worship while the youngsters mingled and chatted each other up. Those rituals have changed nowadays at least among the 'modern' island population but the theory remains unchanged.

If you find yourself here and unsure what to do next, check out Cala D'Albarca which is indisputably one of the most beautiful coves on the island totally unspoilt.

Cova C'an Marça

Breathtaking sea views as you descend steeply to the entrance. Enter this multi-level, yellow-gold world, plotting the smugglers' ancient route with a multilingual guide. Mysteriously, silently over eons, stalagmites and stalagtites have formed into figures, temples and rocket stations. At the heart is a spectacular Music & Light Show with a 30 ft. cascade of diamond-bright water.

Visiting times: Tours hourly from 10.30 a.m till sunset. Open all year.

Cinemas in Ibiza

If you fancy getting out the sun or escaping the madness of the clubs to munch on some popcorn, you should check out one of the many Ibiza Cinemas.

There are several big cinemas around the island where you can catch anything from the latest

Hollywood blockbuster to a lesser known arthouse film. In the more touristy areas you are also likely to find films shown in V.O (versión original) perfect if your Spanish isn't too hot.

Ibiza also holds the annual 'Ibiza and Formentera International Film Festival' a very interesting event if you're into your movies. The festival normally takes place between May and June and attracts actors, directors, scriptwriters and fans from all over the world. Films from Europe, North America, South America, Asia and Africa are nominated each year..

Ibiza Cinemas

Cines Serra

Address: Pg Vara de Rey 6, 07800 Ibiza Town

Tel: (0034) 971 311 471

Multicines Ibiza

Address: Cubells, 07800 Ibiza Town

Tel: (0034) 971 315 211

Cine Regio

Address: Barca 5, 07820 San Antonio de Portmany

Tel: (0034) 971 341 006

Cine Torres

Address: Bisbe Torres 2, 07820 San Antonio de Portmany

Tel: (0034) 971 346 400

Out & About

Ibiza Nightlife

The words 'Ibiza' and 'Nightlife' fit together seamlessly. If you're a nightowl looking for fun and endless entertainment then Ibiza nightlife will be your idea of heaven. In addition to the enormous clubs which can be found on the little island, Ibiza is also home to some world famous bars and some excellent restaurants. So make sure you get the best from Ibiza nightlife with our guide to the island's hottest spots.

Top Ibiza Clubs

Writing a (relatively short) list of the top Ibiza clubs is not an easy task, believe you me. Ibiza clubbing just gets bigger and more extraordinary every summer, transforming itself into a mecca for those in search of a good time. The choice of clubs is endless and the variety within each one is more than you find in the average town! These are not normal clubs, these are the world's most notorious Superclubs and whilst new ones keep popping up, golden oldies like Pacha and Amnesia do not fall from favour but instead keep adding new facilities and attractions. Ibiza clubbing is most certainly not for the faint hearted, so get your energies up and get ready for the party of your life.

Every year sees the hottest dj's on the international circuit kicking up a storm in the world's most infamous club nights. Therefore, you need to choose the music, dj and promoter you want to see and find out what clubs it corresponds to and which night. And you may have a hard time choosing. Every mega club night imaginable from Manumission, Kissdafunk, Twice as Nice and Ministry of Sound to Cream, Release Yourself, Garlands and Gatecrasher can be found doing the rounds in Ibiza's top clubs. Hundreds of PR reps hand out flyers around Ibiza's bars during the evenings to promote the various events this is the best moment to try and pick up discounted entry. If you know where you're going it's worth buying tickets in advance but expect to pay between €30-

€60 for entry to clubs and between €8-€12 per drink when you get inside.

Check out our lowdown of the top Ibiza clubs... now you just need to choose which one to start with!

Amnesia

Opened in 1976, Amnesia is one of Ibiza's oldest clubs. It used to be an open air beauty but now you can dance the night away on the 'terrace' which is actually encapsulated in glass. One of the hottest sound systems on the island, you will find a fair amount of techno and house being busted out in Amnesia.

Located between Ibiza Town and San Antonio de Portmany
Address: Carretera Ibiza a San Antonio a 5km, 07800
Tel: (0034) 971 198 041

Eden

A recent addition to the San An club circuit, Eden is yet to become as legendary as other top Ibiza clubs, but we believe it has potential. With room for some 5,000 gyrating bodies, there is plenty of atmosphere. With respect to music, Eden has not stuck to one style enough to get a reputation, so check the flyers to see what's on.

Located in San Antonio de Portmany
Address: C/Salvador Espriu, 07820
Tel: (0034) 971 803 240

El Divino

One of the newer haunts in the Ibiza club scene, El Divino was opened in 1992 as Ibiza's most exclusive club. Whilst it does now welcome non-VIPs, its small capacity (in Ibiza terms) of 1500 means it's a good choice if you're looking for a (slightly) less raucous experience. El Divino is definitely a hotspot for dancing the night away to some classic house tunes.

Located in San Antonio de Portmany
Address: Passeig Joan Carlos I. 07800
Tel: (0034) 971 318 338

Es Paradis

An Ibiza old timer, Es Paradis has proudly blessed the San Antonio harbour since 1975 and continues to be one of the top Ibiza clubs. Playing the most varied selection of music in Ibiza, Es Paradis made San Antonio what it is today. Whilst it is not the trendiest spot on the island and its fake Romanesque interior makes you feel like you should've worn your best toga for the evening, Es Paradis is filled with a fun loving crowd and you are guaranteed a good time.

Located in San Antonio de Portmany

Address: C/Salvador Espriu 2, 07820

Tel: (0034) 971 346 600

Pacha

When Pacha first opened across the bay from the bustling bars of the port area some opined Ricardo Urguell's creation wouldn't last because it was too far away from the action. They must feel stupid now. Today Pacha is surrounded by apartment blocks, bars, a casino and hotels including El Hotel, which Pacha made their own in 2003.

Avenida Ocho de Agosto, opposite the Marina in Ibiza Town. 10 15 minutes walk from the Port (depending on the quantity of pre-club drinks consumed ;-)

Pacha became famous throughout the world as a haven for glamorous hippies and indeed Ricardo's son Piti's Flower Power production still wows them on occasional Sundays.

When the electronic music revolution hit, house music took over though in recent years they have branched out into hip hop and r'n'b. It's a change of pace and style but they are bonded by their mutual love of the bling.

If you like Spanish pop you can find that too just hang a left into Pachacha after you enter through the front door. Then there's the El Cielo or the Funky Room, where jazzy house, soul, and funk predominate.

Erick'n'TommyThe main room can be quite banging by 5am where you're likely to find big name jocks like Erick Morillo (right, with his mate Tommy Lee), Roger Sanchez, Pete Tong, David Morales, Deep Dish, Danny Tenaglia or Sander

Kleinenberg. If it all gets too much try the soothing sounds on the outside terrace.

The residents include Australian born Sarah Main, Barcelona-born Angel Linde, and hip houser Andy B.

As you've probably gathered from the music description, there are many different zones and bars, each with their own unique vibe. Although an enormous club, with a capacity for over 3000, Pacha still retains a very cosy and intimate feel. Pacha is the only club to open all year round.

Expect to pay from 30€ to 60€ for most nights, the price increases as the island gets busier and the parties get more popular. A Vodka Lemon costs approx. 12€ and a beer 10€..

Located in Ibiza Town
Address: Avenida 8 de Agosto, 07800
Tel: (0034) 971 313 612

Privilege

Privilege was opened in 1978 under the name of Ku when it worked in close competition with the island's earliest clubs. As Pacha had already popularised Ibiza Town and had brought San Antonio fame and fortune, Privilege (or Ku) joined Amnesia on the road between the island's two focal points, giving clubbers another reason to stop between towns. Privilege prides itself on being the world's largest club and with 20 bars, a pool and space for 10,000 people we don't doubt that claim for a second. Probably the only club to have a map at the entrance, it is easy to get lost in Privilege, but even if you do you are sure to stumble upon something cool as you wander around, be it a swimming pool or the club's very own live music venue. You need to be into your hard, serious clubbing music to get the most out of Privilege as most nights showcase some of the world's top trance or techno DJ's.

Located between Ibiza Town and San Antonio de Portmany.
Address: C/Ibiza, 07800
Tel: (0034) 971 198 160

Space

In the grand scheme of Ibiza clubs, Space was a late arrival. Nonetheless, after opening in 1989 the club shot to super stardom by offering clubbers something they had never had before daytime partying in Ibiza. Space began by opening in the mornings and offering true party animals the chance to dance all day. The infamous terrace meant you could still make the most of the sun and it is now home to one of the world's fattest sound systems. But dancing all day wasn't enough for some people and Space discovered that to comply with Spanish law they only had to close for two hours a day. This discovery gave rise to the birth of 22 hour clubbing for the real hardcore ravers. You can expect to hear a mixture of music at Space, from funky house on the terrace to techno tunes inside. Space's opening and closing parties are must-sees and no trip to Ibiza is complete without a visit to Space on a Sunday.

Located near to Ibiza Town
Address: Carre Carbo des 2, Platja d'en Bossa
Tel: (0034) 971 315 127

Pacha Ibiza

Even if you are a first time visitor to the White Island, Pacha is a unlikely to be a foreign name to you. This legendary club chain made its mark on Ibiza in 1973 and set the standard for every club that would follow. Having had great success with their first club in Sitges (opened in 1967), the

Pacha team chose Ibiza for their next big investment and have gone on to open 20 more clubs all over the world.

Pacha Ibiza: Music

Although it is renowned as a House music hotspot, Pacha also has an experimental 'global' room, a funk room, a Spanish music room (in the aptly named 'Pachachá') and a chill out terrace. Recent years have also seen the arrival of r'n'b and hip hop in Pacha so there is plenty of choice for you and the 3000 other clubbers. Plus, if you're peckish you can enjoy the club's very own fusion cuisine restaurant.

Pacha Ibiza is also a good choice if you're planning to visit outside of high season as it is the island's only super club to be open all year long.

Where is it?

Located in Ibiza town, the island's first club was not expected to do very well by the locals. Nonetheless, in the three and a half decades which followed its arrival, Ibiza has transformed into a clubber's paradise and one of Europe's most popular holiday destinations. The no-man's land that Pacha opened up in is now surrounded by bars, restaurants, apartment blocks and hotels, including Pacha's own uber-luxurious suites, perfect if you're looking for designer accommodation, a stone's throw from the island's most infamous club (see www.elhotelpacha.com).

Address: Avenida 8 de Agosto, 07800

Tel: (0034) 971 313 612

Ibiza Bars

If you're looking for a nice cold cocktail on a warm summer's night you will never be far from an Ibiza bar. As well as the cosy locales characteristic all over Spain, Ibiza is also home to some of the world's most famous bars. We've got the lowdown on all the best Ibiza bars so you don't miss a thing!

Ibiza Bar Guide

In Ibiza Town you will find a whole host of good bars and the Sa Penya district is generally where it's at. Make sure you dedicate some time to exploring the Carrer de Barcelona, Carrer de Garijo Cipriano and the Plaça des Parc, where the bars are plentiful.

Bliss

One of the most atmospheric spots on the plaza, definitely worth stopping off at.
Address: Plaça des Parc

Bar Mambo

Not to be confused with San An's legendary Café Mambo, this cool bar is not as famous but a great place to kick start your night at.

Address: Carrer de Garijo Cipriano 10

Lola's Club

One of Ibiza's original hotspots from the 80's, Lola's club has been revamped and renovated ready for the 21st century.

Address: Vía de Alfonso XII 10

Dôme

Classy drinkery ever popular with Ibiza's gay scene.

Address: Via de Alfonso XII 5

Bora Bora

Just outside Ibiza Town, this is undoubtedly the island's most famous beach bar. Open all day andwell into the night you can party to your heart's content at the same time as sunbathing and taking a dip.

Address: Platja d'en Bossa

The other hotspot for Ibiza bars is San Antonio de Portmany and the town's infamous Sunset Strip. Follow the hoards of cocktail lovers and grab yourself a spot on the terrace of one of the island's best bars. This is undoubtedly the place to get your party started with a collection of party loving companions. Most of the bars open mid afternoon and close around 4am when the clubs start hotting up.

Café del Mar

Need we even give a description of this world famous drinkery? Attracting the best DJ's, giving rise to an amazing CD collection and maintaining its reputation as the home of chill-out, no trip to Ibiza would be complete without stopping in Café del Mar.

Address: Calle de Vara del Rey

Tel: (0034) 971 342 516

Café Mambo

This is the hotspot for the Pacha pre-club party and a must if you are doing the rounds along the sunset strip.

Tel: (0034) 971 346 638

Savannah Café

Another great spot to kick start your night with a party loving crowd.

Address: Carrer del General Balanzat 38

Tel: (0034) 971 348 031

Amnesia

Amnesia has blown minds for decades. The house where Amnesia now stands was built at the end of the 18th century. Sold to an aristocratic and artistic widow in the 70s it became a home to hippies who played in bands and danced till dawn while experimenting with LSD and "touching the heavens", according to the Amnesia web site.

In 1975 Spain's long ruling dictator Franco died. In 1976 the new tennant Antonio Escohotado turned the house into a discotheque and christened it Amnesia.

The four four thump of disco took over from rock and is yet to relinquish its hold. But it was the juxtapostion of new and old sounds, pop and underground which was truly influential. Argentine Alfredo Fiorito wowed Paul Oakenfold, Danny Rampling and others in the summer of '88 and let flow a torrent of mass tourism which continues raging to this day.

Half way between Ibiza and San Antonio on the main road, on the opposite side of the highway from the village of San Rafael.

While the previously open air venue was enclosed, Amnesia promoters lost the air of freedom but gained volume. All the successful promoters that inhabit it today have taken advantage of the ability of the sound system to fill every corner of the room with physical waves of sound.

From the sonic innovations of Cocoon's techno-tastic Monday nighter to the euphoric rushes of Cream, it's music made to be felt as much as heard. Typically it's housier on the terrace and more banging in the sala principal.

The terrace is a huge greenhouse with palm trees, many bars and a pleasantly air-conditioned VIP area which encircles the club on the upper floor. The plebs below are cooled by less subtle means two massive "ice cannons" blasting cold air fire off at regular intervals. Amnesia also host Espuma parties at which life-threatening quantities of foam are pumped onto the dance floor in the main room.

Boulder-sized stacks of speakers litter the floor and

are usually colonised by enthusiastic ravers. Tacky dancers bounce around on podiums on the upstairs floor, level with the dj booth which looks down on the writhing masses below.

Eden

Back in the murky 90s a venue called the Star Club morphed into Kaos and then just as swiftly became the present day Eden in the winter of '99/2000.

Eden appropriated the symbol of the competition directly across Es Paradis's apple and a feud was born. The constant bickering keeps them on their toes however as both vie for the custom that pours in from the West End and the other drinking zones of San Antonio and its surrounds.

Judge Jules was a consultant in the design of the dj booth and the Radio 1 jock also occupies the club on Sundays for Eden's highest profile night.

Directly on the waterfront of San Antonio, opposite the harbour. Perfect for town-based clubbing. If you are staying down the Bay (Port d'es Torrent), the disco bus ferries clubbers back and forth all night.

Eden have yet to develop a solid line up and so the music program is in a state of flux. However anthemic trance fans are well served with the aformentioned Julius O'Riordan and colleague, Dave Pearce.

Funky house is on offer when Garlands and Dusted are in the building. R'n'b and hip hop have also been attempted with varying degrees of success. Retro caters for the old skool rave market.

Try the back room on any night for alternative sounds. Electric Sex's gigs are the pick of the bunch.

The sound system is powerful, the lighting effects are reasonably good and there are plenty of bars to service the approximately 5,000 that can be accommodated inside.

Downstairs the dancefloor is separated into two sunken areas with the booth overlooking both. A stage at the far end can also be utilised should Girls Aloud or other such pop groups drop by. In the rear of the club is the glassed back room with capacity for a few hundred.

Upstairs is the restricted access VIP area complete with couches and more bars which overlooks the rest of the club. The design is stark and slightly cold.

El Divino

El Divino was built in 1992 but was open only to a select clientele in its early years. Later it threw open its doors to the general public and became a more intimate alternative to its more high profile neighbour, Pacha.

Over the years the 1,500 capacity venue has hosted a number of promoters looking to dip a toe into the shark-infested Ibiza party pool. Some who have thrived in its environs such as Defected and Roger Sanchez's Release Yourself made the move to Pacha, thus attracting accusations of poaching.

A cloud hangs over El Divino's future due to proposals to demolish the pier it currently sits on the make way for further development of the marina.

Right on the harbour, directly opposite the port where all the shopping and late night festivities take place.

Off Paseo Maritimo, if you're coming by car but our tip is to arrive in style by catching a boat from Ibiza harbour directly to the the club cool huh?

Shiny, happy house mostly, with a bit of a poppy hip hop and r'n'b on the side. The UK's Miss Moneypenny's is a long time partner and recently took over the Friday night slot. Hed Kandi, Salvacion, Azuli and San Francisco's Om Records have also made El Divino their summer home.

It's designed to appeal to the yachting crowd who moor within a champagne cork's pop of the front door. The decor is faux ornate but don't look too closely because it could really use a spruce up. There's one main dance floor with space for a few hundred with a slightly cramped-looking dj booth at the foot of stairs which lead to the interior VIP.

However it's the outside terrace which is the big draw card. It runs the length of the club and every seat has a fantastic view of D'Alt Vila, the castle which has justifiably been granted World Heritage status. The waves lap against the rocks below and there are few better places to enjoy a vodka limon.

Expect to pay from 25€ to 40€ for the big parties, depending on the month. A Vodka Lemon costs approx. 10€ and a beer 7€. Reduced price flyers are available. Taxi fares will be refunded for a group of 3 or more people arriving at the club. Take the receipt with you.

Es Paradis

Second only in longevity to Pacha, Es Paradis opened in 1975. The spectacular creation of Pepe Aguirre drew people to the then sleepy fishing village of San Antonio. Es Paradis have hosted their share of hip parties but as the resort town became dominated by unsophisticated British holidaymakers so the nightlife on offer has gone down market. Modern-day Es Paradis is popular with youngsters based in San An but fails to draw crowds from further afield.

Directly on the waterfront of San Antonio, opposite the harbour. It's only a 5 minute walk from the West End! If you are staying down the Bay (Port d'es Torrent), the disco bus ferries clubbers back and forth all night.

As is usual in Ibiza the music varies from night to night and promoter to promoter, though Es Paradis showcases a greater variety than most. There's the fluffiest of trance courtesy of Dj Sammy, hard dance, old skool, urban sounds in the main room from the long-running Twice As Nice, and funky house at other times.

Quite unique in Ibiza, the decor is largely white and ornate. Think Roman columns and marble surfaces. The greenery is well-maintained and extensive. The main dance floor is round and tiered, and overlooked by the dj booth. Above the dance floor is podium populated by professional exhibitionists.

here are numerous levels and bars and another room for alternative sounds which runs virtually the length of the west wall.

Privilege

In 1978 the venue known as Club Rafael was bought by three Basques. One of their number was the famous footballed Jose Antonio Santamaria. They changed the name of the club to Ku after the nighterie they already owned in San Sebastian.

Throughout the 80s the soon-to-be legend was born and suckled. In 1987 Queen's Freddie Mercury dueted with rival diva opera singer Montserrat Caballe for a tv show broadcast round the world.

In 1990 a roof was added, lierally bringing to a close an era of outdoor partying. In 1991 this roof collapsed during a storm and after refurbishments and much speculation it became Privilege. The arrival of Manumission in 1996 heralded the modern age of imported promoters, guest artists and mass club tourism.

Half way between Ibiza and san Antonio on the main road, near San Rafael. Tricky to miss, given its massive height, girth and garish lighting.

Like most venues in Ibiza it depends on the promoter on the given night. Manumission do popular rave music in the sala principal, provided by both djs and live bands. They also crank up dedicated live venue the Music Box for their Friday party, and incorporate a much-mashed mish mash of rock, house, electro and pop in the others.

Otherwise it ranges from harder, faster sounds of techno and trance to happy clappy house.

If it's your first time in Privilege you're highly likely to get lost. It's extremely easy to get separated from your friends and not see them again till the sun comes up. Don't worry tho, you'll make new ones.

Upon entering the club you go down a massive staircase. You are now are bang in the middle of one of the world's largest dancefloors. At its centre the dj is suspended above a swimming pool . At the far end is a stage where girls and boys dance around in varying stages of undress and a show with a non-linear dramatic structure (i.e. it's confusing) takes place.

Above this room is a the large lattice dome which supports the Privilege sign. To the left is a multi-level terraced chill out area. Downstairs is a toilet complete with dj booth. To the right (south) is the gayer-than-average Coco Loco. In the far corner is the aforementioned Music Box. There's a map on a sign out the front.

Expect to pay up to 60€ for Manumission. Other nights vary between 20€ and 50€. There are often free tickets in Ibiza Town and San Antonio for the lesser known promoters' nights. A vodka limon costs approx. 10€ and a beer 8€.

Space

In 1989 a concert hall in Ibiza became the home for the concept the whole world knows as Space. Truly Balearic in its original incarnation, Pepe Rosello's program included live bands, flamenco shows and exciting electronic music.

One of its inspired innovations was opening in the morning, after the other clubs had shut. This, in conjunction with the introduction of music onto the terrace by raconteurs extraordinaire Alex P and Brandon Block, caused a sensation.

The reaction was so intense that a decision was made to extend the hours still further and now Sunday is the biggest day of the week in Ibiza. Expect to roll out at dawn on Monday.

The success was contagious and music lovers now flock to Space for different nights from leading lights such as Carl Cox, Manumission, La Troya, Matinee and more.

Next to the Waterslide Park in Playa d'en Bossa. 5 Minutes by taxi from Ibiza Town

From the sublime to the very hard. Funky Balearic house on the Sunset Terrace, where you can sip Vodka Lemons in the sun and chill out with Ibiza's wildest clubbers. On the upstairs premier etage you can hear left-field beats and soulful classics and inside the dirtiest techno wickedness. A fabulous contrast programme, headed both inside and out by the world's finest DJs.

Space enjoys something approaching cult status on the world dance scene. Dedicated clubbers fly in especially for the opening and closing parties at which an outside stage is set up especially, and many world class DJs name Space as their favourite club. It is located right under the flight path of planes landing at Ibiza's only airport. As the jets come swooping in everyone there and on the Sunset Terrace throws their arms to the sky and screams.

The Terrace of old is unrecognisable. A booming sound system has been installed, necessitating its enclosure by glass but allowing a 6am close time. Inside the Discoteca the art of sonics has been taken to a new level. It's clairty and power makes djs drool. The lighting will make your jaw hit the floor.

Upstairs more alternative sounds can be explored in the Caja Roja (Red Box) and the aforementioned Premier Etage.

Space has great Djs, cool clubbers, and is open when everywhere else is shut. Highly recommended.

Expect to pay from 30 € to 60 € for the the Sunday Sessions, depending on the month. Entry on other days costs between 30 € and 40 €. A Vodka Lemon costs 10 € and a beer 8 €.

Ibiza Restaurants

If you're looking for good food then you're in for a treat with Ibiza's restaurants. The main thing to avoid are the very over touristed areas where quality takes second place to serving the masses quickly and cheaply. The somewhat tacky beachside restaurants that you may find in San Antonio de Portmany or Santa Eularia are what many visitors to the island think sums up Ibiza food . However, there are many great Ibiza restaurants to be discovered, from exclusive eateries to traditional tapas bars. Most of the top Ibiza clubs like Pacha and El Divino also have their own restaurants, meaning you don't even have to leave the clubs to eat!

Many restaurants close on Mondays so it's worth ringing beforehand to be sure. Check out our listings for the island's best spots:

Ibiza Restaurants Listings

Bar San Juan

Family run, traditional Spanish cuisine

Address: Carrer de Guillem de Montgri 8, Ibiza

Town

Tel: (0034) 971 31 16 03

Cala Mastella

Exquisite fish restaurant hidden away in this secluded cove you must book in person the day before you plan to eat there.

Address: Cala Mastella, near Santa Eularia.

Ca'n Alfredo

Popular with the locals, this is the perfect place to try some traditional fare.

Address: Passeig de Vara de Rey 16, Ibiza Town

Tel: (0034) 971 311 274

El Ayoun

Tasty moroccan cuisine in this stylishly designed restaurant-come-chill out lounge. A favourite with clubbed out clubbers make sure you reserve.

Address: Carre d'Isidor Macabich, San Rafael,

between Ibiza Town and San Antonio de Portmany.
Tel: (0034) 971 198 335

El Naranjo

Brilliant seafood in a pretty setting.

Address: Carrer de Sant Josep, Santa Eularia

Tel: (0034) 971 330 324

Es Boldadó

Perfect views and seafood in this lovely restaurant.

Address: Cala d'Hort, southwest Ibiza near San José

Tel: (0034) 626 494 537

Es Xarcu

You may think this is just a beach bar but Es Xarcu serves up some of the best seafood in Ibiza

Address: Cala es Xarcu. 9km from Sant Josep de Talaia, 13.5km from Ibiza Town.

Tel: (0034) 971 187 867

La Brasa

Great mediterranean fusion cuisine with a beautiful terrace.

Address: C/Pere Sala 3, Ibiza Town

Tel: (0034) 971 301 202

La Vitoria

Tasty, traditional cuisine

Address: C/Riambau 1, Ibiza Town

Tel: (0034) 971 310 622

Las Dalias

From a traditional tapas bar to cellar restaurant, pizzeria and tea shop, this place has got it all. It also houses the Saturday hippy market of the same name.

Address: Carretera San Carlos Km 12, 97840

Nearest Towns: Santa Eularia and Es Cana

Tel: (0034) 971 326 825 / www.lasdalias.es

Sa Capella

A romantic getaway just outside San An, Sa Capella is the perfect spot to enjoy quality seafood whilst gazing into your loved one's eyes.

Address: San Antonio de Portmany, 07840

Tel: (0034) 971 340 057

S'Ametller

One of Ibiza's most highly acclaimed restaurants, this is the place to go for gourmet experimental cuisine in Ibiza town.

Address: Carrer de Pere Francesc 12, Ibiza Town

Tel: (0034) 971 311 780

Ibiza Shopping

Shopaholic? In search of souvenirs? you'll find what you're looking for when shopping in Ibiza.

If you are looking to shop till you drop in trendy boutiques or cheap and cheerful clothes shops then your best bet is to get down to Sa Penya in Ibiza town. It is quite incredible that as well as having a vast array of class bars, it is also home to some great shops. The perfect place to do your Ibiza shopping.

However, if you're in search of a real bargain or something made locally in Ibiza then you can explore the island's infamous hippy markets. There are markets throughout the week so you can be sure to catch one of them. The biggest and most popular are in Es Cana and Las Dalias.

Ibiza Shopping: Las Dalias Hippy Market

This market is fairly sizeable with a good range of stalls. It is one of the most authentic in Ibiza and runs year round, rather than just as a summer time tourist pleaser. Set in one of Ibiza's coolest restaurants, Las Dalias is a rainbow coloured maze of market stalls. Local artesans are keen to sell you their handicrafts but you can also pick up music and clothes at this excellent little market. Be warned though it is a popular choice, so if you don't fancy facing the crowds pop along to the smaller version on Monday nights.

Where? San Carles de Peralta, nearest big towns: Santa Eularia and Portinatx
When? Saturdays 10am-20pm (summer), 10am-18pm (winter)
Monday Evenings.

Ibiza Shopping: Es Cana Hippy Market

This is Ibiza's biggest hippy market and it happens every Wednesday during the summer. The truth be known this hippy market is a long way from what it was in the seventies when flower power was truly the order of the day. But whilst the Es Cana market has become somewhat commercialised and tourist orientated, that does not mean it is not the perfect place to pick up some souvenirs. You can buy pretty much anything from gold and silver, trinkets and textiles to jewellery, arts and leather goods. Despite the influx of tourists, shopping here feels quite relaxed due to the soft beat of bongos courtesy of the 'hippies'.

When? Every Wednesday from May through October, 9.30am-19pm
Where? Punta Arabí, Es Cana, just north from Santa Eularia

Ibiza Sports

When you've seen all the cultural sights or tired of the clubs, there is no better way to make the most of your holiday than to have a go at some Ibiza sport. With the sun overhead and the warm waters, Ibiza is the perfect destination to enjoy watersports, but similarly heading inland or away from the tourist filled beaches will be a rewarding experience on the White Island. Click on the following links to find out more about Ibiza sport.

Tennis

Fabulous weather and long summer days are perfect for tennis enthusiasts. Many tennis courts are scattered around the island, and many hotels have their own courts for hotel guests. Ask at your hotel reception for information about courses and tournaments. Also visit Club de Campo Ibiza's largest tennis club.

Mountainbike

Because of the narrow country roads and the dangerous mix of drivers in summer, please be very careful when out mountain biking. Although there are bike rental shops, if you place importance on good quality equipment, it is best to bring your own bike. Most airlines will transport bikes free of charge when given appropriate notice. in some cases a small charge will be made.

Golf

As an alternative to the great variety of nautical sports available in Ibiza, the Golf Club of Ibiza is there for all those who wish to play the sport at the same time as enjoying the clean air and enviable climate of Ibiza, in which the practice of this sport can take place in both the summer and winter seasons. Throughout the year, different tournaments are held, where fans can measure their talents on the greens.

Horse riding

There are over five horsemanship schools on the island. Horse riding is a big thing here. The horse is a very well respected animal and horsemanship is an integral part of the island's history and culture.

Water Sports in Ibiza

If you want to make the most of Ibiza's beautiful coastline then you should check out the possibilities for water sports in Ibiza. Whilst many people are content with a quick dip in the sea, some of us prefer to get our adrenaline racing with some sports. The great thing about Ibiza is that there is something for everyone. Whilst the quieter, more secluded Ibiza beaches make up for in tranquility what they lack in amenities, the larger beaches are buzzing day and night with activities to suit all ages.

Rent a pedalo for some beach relaxation or jet around the port on a banana boat or donut. You can easily have a go at waterskiing or parasailing in the bigger resorts or ofcourse, there is always a traditional bit of swimming.

Windsurfing

There is rarely enough wind for planing conditions in the high season (but easily enough for beginners). In early and late summer, the South wind (Scirroco) can pick up to a good force 4 once a week, and the West wind (Mistral) sometimes comes howling in at force 6. The most popular beaches are Cala Martina, Cala Conta and Playa d'en Bossa. Of these, Cala Martina is the easiest to surf with plenty of flat and shallow water. Playa d'en bossa is all sand, but choppy when the South wind blows directly onshore. Cala Conta is for the more advanced surfer, and is trickier to get in and out. A shorty will be enough in the high season months of July, August and September (also gives good protection from the sun). For earlier and later months, as well as winter, think about taking a longer wetsuit, especially for the legs.

Diving

Warm, clear waters and over 200 kilometres of spectacular coastline make Ibiza a popular resort for both amateur and professional divers, almost the whole year round. There are many excellent and qualified diving schools located around the island offering courses from Beginner up to Advanced. Dive locations include cave dives and wreck dives. The water is particularly clear around Ibiza.

Ibiza Adventure Sports

If you're looking for some high adrenaline fun outside of the clubs then why not have a go at some Ibiza adventure sports?

Whether a challenging hike around the island is up your street or trotting along on horseback sounds more your kind of thing, you can be guaranteed to have fun and see Ibiza in a different light.

Hike in Ibiza, Spain

Hiking in Ibiza, Spain can give you a totally different view of the island. Instead of sticking with the tourists in resorts or touring the island by car, why not get out there on foot and breathe in the sea air? It's a truly refreshing way to enjoy Ibiza that many people miss out on. There are various different routes you can take depending on your ability (and stamina!) so just make sure you choose one that suits you.

Global Spirit organises guided hikes around the island which vary in difficulty, many of which comb the prettiest parts of the Ibizan coastline..

If you prefer to organise your own hikes then the northern area of Portinatx comes highly recommended for hiking in Ibiza, Spain. The craggy cliffs which line the coast here make for excellent walking with some tremendous views. Starting in the town there are some 10km to reach Punta Xarraca and when you get there you can enjoy Cala Xarraca, one of the most lovely Ibiza beaches.

A more straightforward hike would be to tour the coastline along the west of the island from Cala de Bou at San Antonio de Portmany along to the absolutely beautiful Playas de Comte.

Those of you with a bit more energy could power up one of Ibiza's highest peaks. The inland hike from San Jose to Sa Talaia takes around 4 hours each way and offers some lovely views of the island.

If you are planning to hike in Ibiza, Spain during the summer, make sure you wear plenty of suncream, bring clothes to cover up from the sun and plenty of water.

Trips from Ibiza

Travel to Formentera

So, you've partied till dawn in Ibiza and just want a bit of peace and quiet away from the masses? Look no further, it takes a mere 30 minutes to travel to Formentera by boat and this little gem of an island is just what you need to recharge those batteries when you've run out of steam.

Formentera is not as isolated and undeveloped as it once was, but the lack of totally colonised areas packed with highrises and the authenticity of the restaurants makes a refreshing change to other parts of the mediterranean coast. Formentera was left uninhabited between the fifteenth and seventeenth centuries and even today with its population of around 8000, it is easy to find yourself a quiet spot to chill out in.

Much of the island is closed during the winter, but between May and October is springs to life and cool beach bars, excellent fish restaurants and the few accommodation options open their doors to the summer time visitors. Unlike the other Balearics, Formentera tends to be more popular with Italians rather than Brits and Germans. The Italian idea of a good time tends to revolve less around getting slaughtered which results in a far more relaxed holiday ambience. Tourism is an important industry in Formentera, especially in Es Pujols, however, developers are sympathetic to the aesthetic beauty of the island and it is relatively easy to avoid the more touristy areas if your heart so desires.

The main thing to do in Formentera is relax. With only one club and a splattering of bars, it is the perfect destination if you want to get away from it all, enjoy good food, clear waters, long sandy beaches and pretty pine forests. Sound like your cup of tea? Travel to Formentera and experience it for yourself.

Travel to Formentera: Highlights

Beaches You cannot beat Formentera's beaches if you're looking for a little dose of the Caribbean in Europe. The island's boho 'anything go's' attitude is commonplace in Formentera's beach culture and many people sunbathe in the nude all over the island. For a natural facial head to the Illa S'Espalmador, a miniature islet just off the island. Totally uninhabited you can truly make the most of uncommercialised beach life here and bathe in the mud baths if you feel like revitalising your skin. Just back on Formentera's mainland you can also revel in the gogreous stretches of white sand that characterise Platja de ses Illetes and Platja de Llevant. Heading down south you will find another great collection of beaches known as the Platja de

Migjorn. For amenities, hotels and a bit more commercialisation head to the east or western points of the bay. Stick in the middle and sip a cocktail at the beach Bar if you want to keep things au naturale.

Peace Out Just as the hippies hit Ibiza in the 60's, Formentera also became a hotspot for flower power and boho collectives. Unlike Ibiza however, Formentera continues to thrive in this way (and not just for the benefit of the tourists). This laid back mentality is addictive and the best way to enjoy travelling to Formentera is to take a leaf out the hippies book and chill.

The Great Outdoors Formentera is an easily manageable, almost entirely flat terrain and it is perfect for exploring by bike. Numerous places hire scooters and bikes out and it is a much greener option than hiring a car (spanning only 20km from east to west means that's hardly worth doing anyway). Cylcing is a great way to get out there and discover hidden beaches and isolated corners of the island. Also, the perfect coastline offers some photo-worthy views making Formentera a great place to walk around. You won't get the same kind of testing hikes as in Ibiza or Mallorca but nonetheless, it is a pleasant way to spend an afternoon.

Sant Francesc Xavier The capital of Formentera, this attractive town is overflowing with picture perfect white washed houses and great traditional little eateries. Located 4km inland, it is a good place to explore if you fancy getting away from the beaches and soaking up the laid back vibe in the most relaxed urban centre known to man. The 18th century fortress and 14th century chapel are worth taking a peek at too.

Travel to Mallorca

Once you've made the most of Ibiza, you may want to explore the capital of the Balearics and travel to Mallorca. There are regular Balearic Island ferries to make the journey quick and simple and on a fast ferry it takes just 2 hours between islands.

Mallorca is not only the autonomous capital but is also the largest island in the Balearics with a long standing cultural heritage and a lot of well preserved traditions. On the one hand, Mallorca is famous for its busy, built up resorts which line much of the coastline and are inundated with German and British sun-seekers every summer. Whilst on the other hand, Mallorca also contains thriving Spanish cities, charming towns, an impressive mountain range and idyllic landscapes. Such diversity within 3640 km² means that travelling to Mallorca is an exciting and memorable trip for any visitor and shouldn't be missed!

Travel to Mallorca: Highlights

Palma de Mallorca A million miles from the package tourist's perception of Mallorca (which tends to consist of German sausages and beer), Mallorca's dazzling capital is a pleasure to explore with a really special vibe. Home to 300,000 people (almost half the island's population), Palma is a buzzy hub of artistic flair with pretty building lining every corner, great museums and an addictive ambience. The main attraction is the massive gothic cathedral which can be seen from all over Palma, it's carefully carved, sandy coloured exterior making a wonderful backdrop to the city. Inside you will find some surprisingly modern touches added by Barcelona's architectural legend, Antonio Gaudi. Also worth seeing are two palaces, the Palau March and Palau de l'Almudaina and the new Contemporary Art Museum is well worth a visit. You could easily fill a few days in Palma as after you've seen the tourist hotspots there are endless bars and restaurants to enjoy. Dining along the waterfront by night and gazing p at the spot-lit cathedral as you sip a glass of wine is an unbeatable holiday highlight.

Serra de Tramuntana If you travel to the north of Mallorca you will find the dramatic craggy cliff faces of the Sierra de Tramuntana. This is the most wonderful place to head if you enjoy hiking as the landscapes are raw and undeveloped, giving you a real sense of freedom. Trails vary in difficulty so make sure you attempt one suited to your ability and avoid long walks in the height of the summer when temperatures reach boiling point. You can also dip in and out of traditional villages or find hidden coves in this less developed quart of the island.

Parc Natural de S'Albufera Wildlife fanatics should head straight to this extremely pleasant reserve where you can admire a wide range of flora and fauna. In particular, bird lovers will be in their element with over 200 species fluttering around the park.

Hillside Villages If highrise hotels aren't your style you will be in heaven with Mallorca's array of charming little villages tucked away amidst the hills. Sóller is a popular choice and the best place to stay if you plan to hike around the Serra de Tramuntana. Deià is another popular choice and has visitors enchanted time and again, it also has one of the prettiest bays on the island, the Cala de Deià. Head to Pollença for some excellent island vistas from the hilltop chapel and some souvenir shopping at the Sunday market. Also, make time to drop in on the impressive monasteries at Valldemossa and Lluc.

Beaches Last but not least, one of the main draws to Mallorca, and indeed all the Balearics, is the huge number of beaches. Mallorca alone has 550km of glorious coastline so whether you are looking for busy beaches with watersports and bars or a chilled out cove to laze around in, you'll find it somewhere along the way. Head to the east coast if you're in search of mass tourism. Find glitz and glamour on the southwest coast at Port d'Andratx or Sant Elm and head to the Cala de Sant Vicent if you're want true tranquility.

Travel to Menorca

The second biggest Balearic Island is the beautiful, tranquil haven of Menorca. You can reach it in an hour by ferry from the island of Mallorca and it is a must see if you are planning on hopping around the Balearics. You can also fly from Ibiza to Menorca with Iberia or Air Europa, however, this often involves stopping over and can be quite pricey.

Of all the Balearic Islands, Menorca is the least developed and the second largest, meaning that finding an isolated spot isn't too hard, even in mid-summer. The island is home to some stunning scenery and its slightly wetter climate means that fields and forests stay verdant and luscious looking. There is also over 200km² of rugged coastline to explore and some carefully preserved cities. The real beauty of Menorca is that over 40% is protected by UNESCO as a Biosphere Reserve which ensures that Menorca will continue to be a unique destination in the mediterranean that won't succumb to the effects of mass tourism any time soon.

Travel to Menorca: Highlights

Beaches If you want to discover hidden coves and isolated beaches then head north and explore the most stunning part of Menorca's coastline. You will find craggy cliff faces, clear waters and sandy beaches to relax on, the perfect setting to collect you thoughts and gaze out to sea. Hiring a bike is one of the most pleasant ways to get about and escape the other holidaymakers.

Maó Capital of the island since 1713 when the British decided to move it there, Maó's mish-mashed past is documented in the eclectic architecture which lines its streets. An interesting mixture of Georgian houses and modern Spanish offerings gives the Menorcan capital a touch of originality not found anywhere else in the archipelago. The city is also home to some good museums, pretty plazas, nice churches and a buzzy bar and restaurant scene down by the harbour.

Monte Toro If you want to get some dazzling views of the island and take some holiday snaps worth framing then head to Menorca's highest point, in the centre of the island. It's a 3.2km climb to the top of Monte Toro where pilgrims used to flock year in and year out to the majestic monastery that blessed its summit. Today, you can explore part of the convent which still stands there, but above all this spot is best for sitting back and enjoying the view.

Ciutadella The original capital of Menorca, Ciutadella reined until 1722 and acts as a carefully preserved example of the Spanish influence on the island. Unlike Maó, Ciutadella does not showcase British architecture, but rather, a huge collection of exquisite colonial style mansions.

Talatí de Dalt Archeologists have been baffled by Menorca for many a year. They are unsure of much of the island's early history and have never been able to work out the function of a series of unusual structures found all over the island. T-shaped Taulas and cone shaped Talayots stll remain in various locations on Menorca but the reason for them being there cannot be deciphered. Initially they were considered to be watchtowers but this opinion has not been proved entirely. You can see an impressive example of these in Talatí de Dalt where an enormous Taula and Talayot are enclosed by the remains of a wall in a beautiful area filled with olive trees.

Planning Your Trip

Travel & Transportation

Travel and transportation in Ibiza, Spain is a pleasure for even the most unsure traveller. Whether you are looking to bus it from one end of the island to the other, get on the road with a hire car, island hop around the Balearics or arrive by air, Ibiza, Spain has lots of well run services to make your trip go without any technical hitches.

So what are you waiting for? All you need to know about travel and transportation in Ibiza, Spain is right here click on the relevant links and get ready to jet around the beautiful Balearic islands!

Ibiza Airports

Ibiza Airport (IBZ) is the international gateway where most visitors arrive and is located four-and-a-half miles from Ibiza town. 50-plus carriers fly to the island, although many restrict operations to summer charters. The main airlines operating year-round are Air Berlin, Air Europa, British Airways, and Iberia. British Airways flies from London, while Air Europa has routes from Barcelona and Madrid. Air Berlin connects to Düsseldorf, and Iberia flies to Palma de Mallorca. Americans can get here via a major European hub, such as the UK (London, Birmingham or Manchester) or Spain (Madrid or Barcelona).

As an airport that sees major tourist traffic, IBZ is naturally equipped with bars, restaurants, fast food, ATMs, a post office, and currency exchange booths. A direct bus runs from the airport to Ibiza town every 30 minutes. Other transportation options include private shuttles or taxis, although the latter often apply an airport surcharge of a few extra euros. Those wanting more autonomy can rent a vehicle from the desks in the Arrivals hall.

Cheap Flights to Ibiza

Package deals and budget flights are two of the most common ways to get to Ibiza. Cheap flights to Ibiza can be found from numerous destinations throughout Europe, however, it can get pretty pricey if you're looking to travel from further afield. By far the best value option is to book early and pick up a direct flight to Ibiza. Flights are generally cheaper during the winter months when there is less demand, however, it is worth taking into account that many cheap flight companies only offer flights to Ibiza between May and October. Low cost airlines offer a no frills service which makes travel accesible to everyone. Many cheap flight companies also have seasonal sales, so if you know you're definitely going to Ibiza then keep a regular look out at the following sites and pick up an extra cheap deal.

Check out the following companies for cheap flights to Ibiza:

Air Berlin www.airberlin.com
BMI Baby www.bmibaby.com
Condor www.condor.com
Easyjet www.easyjet.com

Jet 2 www.jet2.com

Monarch Air www.flymonarch.com

SpanAir www.spanair.com

Vueling www.vueling.com

Balearic Island Ferries

Travelling by boat is another popular option and there are several services which run Balearic Island ferries between the islands, as well as to mainland Spain.

Travelling around the Balearic Islands by ferry varies in price depending when you want to go, what speed boat you opt for and how luxurious you want the accommodation to be. If you are travelling from mainland Spain you may often find that it works out more economical to catch a cheap flight to Ibiza, however, ferry may be your best option if you want to island hop.

Balearic Island ferries run more frequently during the summer months (May-October) when there are frequent arrivals and departures between Ibiza (Ibiza Town and San Antonio), Mao (Menorca), Palma (Mallorca) and Formentera.

From mainland Spain most Balearic Island ferries leave from Barcelona (8-11hours depending on type of boat) and Valencia (3.5-6 hours) and Denia on Spain's Costa Blanca (3-5 hours).

There are two well known Balearic Island ferry companies which run services throughout the year, but there is more extensive timetbale during the summer.

Balneària

Ferries connecting Ibiza with Denia, Palma, Barcelona and Formentera.

www.balnearia.com

Trasmediterránea

Ferries connecting Ibiza with Barcelona, Valencia, Maó (Menorca), Palma de Mallorca.

www.trasmediterranea.es

Ibiza Bus Travel

Ibiza bus travel is a straightforward, comfortable and affordable way to see the island.

Whilst many people enjoy the freedom that hiring a car gives them, if you feel unsure on foreign roads and prefer not to spend your time map reading, then you can rely on Ibiza bus travel to get you to your destination. There are several very efficient bus services with regular transportation between Ibiza's biggest cities, great beaches and little towns.

The following companies operate on routes from Ibiza town and various different areas of the island, see the list below to plan your journey and make sure you catch the right bus you can check out timetables and route plans on www.ibizabus.com:

- ✓ Autobuses Lucas Costa
- ✓ Autobuses Empreseas H.F Vilas
- ✓ Autobuses San Antonio
- ✓ Autobuses Voramor El Gauch

Car Hire Ibiza

If you enjoy the freedom that driving gives you then why not consider car hire in Ibiza? There is plenty of choice regarding car rental firms in Ibiza and roads are safe and well signed making it a relatively easy destination to navigate your way round.

A plethora of car hire companies operate around the island with a large choice of vehicles. Whilst most of the larger companies operate from Ibiza airport (very close to Ibiza Town), several have offices in other parts of the island which is worth bearing in mind if you want to pick up and drop off your vehicle at different locations. Car hire in Ibiza is a popular choice with visitors to the island, so you'll do well to book in advance especially if you are visiting during the summer months. All the larger car rental companies have sites where you can often get a discount by booking ahead, also, this means that everything is organised before you even arrive and you'll be free to get behind the wheel as soon as you land!

Check out the following reputable companies for car hire in Ibiza:

Alamo	National
Ibiza Airport	Ibiza Airport
www.alamo.com	www.nationalcar.com
Avis	PepeCar

Ibiza Airport, Santa Eularia , San Antonio de Portmany, Ibiza des Cana, Portinatx www.avis.co.uk	Two locations close to Ibiza Airport www.pepecar.com
Europcar Ibiza Airport, Santa Eularia www.europcar.com	Travel Depot Ibiza Airport, Jose ma Cuadrado, San Antonio de Portmany, Santa Eularia www.traveldepot.co.uk
Hertz Ibiza Airport www.hertz.com	

Car Hire in Ibiza: Safety precautions for driving in Spain.

✓ Make yourself familiar with the Spanish driving laws before you get to Ibiza . British and Australian drivers take time to adapt to driving on the right hand side of the road!

✓ Spanish national fiestas see a huge influx of people taking to the roads which is when the most road accidents occur in Spain, so take extra care on these days.

- ✓ Obviously, drink driving is illegal but the limits are especially low in Spain 0.5 mg of alcohol per millilitre of blood.

- ✓ Speeding can result in on the spot fining so get used to the speed limits:
Motorways: 120 km/ hour
Open Road: 90-100 km/ hour
Town: 50 km/ hour

Ibiza Property & Real Estate

Ibiza is one of Spain's most popular destinations and continues to have one of the most thriving property markets in the country. Whilst the Spanish property 'boom' has slowed on the mainland, in particular along the Costa del Sol, the Balearic islands, continue to be one of the hottest spots for buying Spanish property. Year round good weather and a hugely busy tourist industry means that investing in buy-to-rent Ibiza property is a guaranteed winner due to the high demand for holiday lets. Similarly, those who have bought homes have seen a significant rise in property value as Ibiza steadily maintains its popularity.

Luxury, luxury and more luxury seems to be the order of the day in Ibiza. Rent luxury villas in Ibiza is for celebrities and the rich and famous the standard for building o renting impressive mansions with every kind of luxurious trimming. For the rest of us, prices are multiplying by up to 300% in some areas and it is becoming increasingly hard to find a plot of land to build your own property on. Villas and apartments with sea views tend to be the hottest investments, which is worth bearing in mind when choosing your Ibiza property.

With a little foresight and some careful investigation you could find yourself a winning property in Ibiza. The southwestern areas of the island between Ibiza Town and the holiday resort of San Antonio de Portmany have been popular for a long time and are the most pricey. However, it may be worth checking out the beautiful northern areas surrounding Portinatx, where an isolated spot isn't so hard to come by and there is a lot more scope for finding less inflated property prices.

Check out this list of reputable Ibiza Real Estate Agents and start the search for your dream Ibiza property.

Ibiza Estate Agents

BBS Consulting	Ibiza House Shop
Address: Avenida Cubells 9, apto 164	Address: Calle San Jaime 45, 1°
	E-07840 Ibiza Town
E-07830, Sant Josep	Tel: (0034) 971 303 844

Ibiza Travel Guide Spain

Tel: (0034) 971 800 705 www.bbs-ibiza.com	www.ibizahouseshop.com
Bussard Mediterraneo C/San Jaime 62 E-07840, Ibiza Tel: (0034) 971 331 196 www.bussard-ibiza.com	Ibiza Prestige Avenida Bartolomé Rosello 1 E-07800, Ibiza Town Tel: (0034) 971 190 455 www.ibizaprestige.com
Can Ravell Address: Can Peter Siesta E-07840, Santa Eulalia Tel: (0034) 971 330 626 www.canravell.net	Lider Casa Address: Calle Via Punica 21 bajo E-07800, Ibiza Town Tel: (0034) 971 303 844 www.lidercasa.com
Don Piso Ibiza Town Address: Passatge Castaní 3 E-07800, Ibiza Town Tel: (0034) 971 300 270 www.donpiso.com/ibizacentro	Don Piso San Antonio de Portmany Address: C/Madrid 12, edificio Kabiro, local 2 E-07820, San Antonio de Portmany Tel: (0034) 971 804 894 www.donpiso.com/sanantonio
Engel Völkers Address: Avenida Santa Eulalia 17 E-07800, Ibiza Town Tel: (0034) 971 311 336 Address: Calle Carlos V 12, local 10	

E-07800, Ibiza Town
Tel: (0034) 971 193 445

Address: Calle San Jaime 37
E-07840, Santa Eulalia
Tel: (0034) 971 807 180

www.engelvoelkers.es

If you've got your heart set on investing in an Ibiza property then check out our Spanish Mortgageadvice so you can get the ball rolling as soon as possible.

Spanish Mortgages
Advice for Foreign Buyers
Totally characteristic of the relaxed and laid back way of life in Spain, sorting out a mortgage is not a particularly quick process so if you have decided to invest in a property, it is worth investigating your Spanish mortgage options early on. The good news is, Spain is such a popular destination for foreign

buyers that there are masses of options to help you every step of your purchase. To facilitate foreign buyers many international banks have developed foreign mortgages and now several Spanish banks, like La Caixa have jumped on the bandwagon and offer special services in English.

International Banks with Spanish Mortgages

In addtion to general foreign mortgages, a good handful of international banks now offer special 'Spanish mortgages'. These are specifically catered to the Spanish housing market and deal with every aspect of translation, lawyers and insurance. A godsend for non-Spanish speakers wishing to complete a smooth purchase in Spain! Some of the most reputable international banks are the following:

Banco Santander (Also known as Abbey)

www.gruposantander.es/bprivada/binternational.html

Barclays

www.barclays.co.uk/buyingabroad/

Deutsche Bank

www.db.com

Lloyds TSB

www.lloydstsb.com/mortgages/spanish_mortgages.asp

Natwest

www.natwestinternational.com/spanish.asp

Applying for a Spanish Mortgage

When applying for a mortgage in Spain you must ensure you have the documents listed below:

- ✓ Valid Passport, residence permit or Spanish ID card (NIE)

  Your last three bank statements (account

statement for last three years if you are self-employed)

- ✓ Your last three salary slips.
- ✓ Spanish tax declaration for the last financial year (P60 form in UK) or if you are self-employed you need to provide tax slip for the last two years.
- ✓ New Building: Declaration deed from developer.
- ✓ Resale Properties: Property deeds of current owner.

Luxury Villas in Ibiza

Spending some days in Ibiza is a unique experience... so the house where the visitor stays must also be unique: one that is up to par of the luxuries and experiences that the island may offer.

That is why Luxury Villas Ibiza is a great option, since it offers 4 luxury houses on the best and most exclusive areas of the island. Either you are looking for a modern and avant-garde place, or you wish for a more typical atmosphere, these houses offer a comfortable space that's been cared to detail to assure a pleasant and relaxing stay.

Located on different settings, but each of them with a personal charm, each house is fully equipped with all sorts of facilities and services for your comfort, amongst which a magnificent pool and a security service stand out. Given their location, and whether it is with friends or family, you can enjoy privacy, but also the closeness of the most remarkable spots of interest in Ibiza. This makes the houses of Luxury Villas Ibiza perfect places to plan an excursion... or simply rest looking at the sunset with a marvellous view.

Each location has been chosen with devotion to the island, and with the conscience that a holiday in Ibiza is not like any other vacation, but an exceptional pleasure, something that goes beyond the senses. The moment when the visitor crosses the door he will find a house that can only be found in a magical enviroment, but also warm and cozy: a place that offers us the priviledge of sharing with our closest friends or relatives some days that we won't ever forget.

Spain Visas & Embassies

For members of the European Union (plus Iceland, Norway and Switzerland), Spain visas aren't required, however, if you are planning on staying for an extended period (i.e over 90 days) you should visit your local police station or town hall to get 'Empadronado' (register your address and yourself in Spain). Similarly you should apply for a

NIE number the Spanish government no longer give identity cards to foreigners but they will issue you with a number and certificate which simplifies things when opening a bank account, buying a house, applying for social security etc.

Citizens of many other countries do not need a visa to enter for a stay of less than 90 days: Australia, Canada, Israel, Japan, New Zealand and the US are among them. If you are planning on staying for longer than 90 days, you must check with the Spanish consulate nearest you for the specific conditions of applying for a Spain visa, which can vary depending on your situation.

Student visas are not too difficult to obtain if you can get your programme provides you with the necessary paperwork. Even in this case, however, the process will take at least a month. In order to work in Spain it is necessary to have an official offer from a company in Spain. These types of visas are not easy to get for non-EU citizens.

Most countries' Spanish embassies are located in Madrid, which is easily reachable via plane from the Balearic Islands. However, some countries also have a consulate in the Balearic Islands. You'll find the majority of these consulates located in Palma de Mallorca, although Britain has an additional consulate in Ibiza. Below we have listed the Madrid embassies for English speaking countries, and where applicable, their consulate in the Balearic Islands. Please be aware this list is not exhaustive, so if you do not find your country on the list don't panic just enquire at the Spanish embassy in your country.

Australian Embassy in Madrid	**British Embassy in Madrid**
Plaza Descubridor Diego de OrdÃ¡s 3	Calle Fernando el Santo 16
28003, Madrid	28010, Madrid
Tel: (0034) 91 353 6600	Tel: (0034) 917 008 200

British Consulate in Palma de Mallorca Convent dels Caputxins 4, Edificio Orisba B 4D 07002, Palma de Mallorca Tel: (0034) 971 712 445	**British Consulate in Ibiza** Avenida Isidoro Macabich 45- 1st floor 07800, Ibiza Tel: (0034) 971 301 818
Canadian Embassy in Madrid NuÃ±Ã©z de Balboa 35 28001, Madrid Tel: (0034) 914 233 250	**Irish Embassy in Madrid** Paseo de la Castellana 46-4 28046 Madrid Tel: (0034) 91 436 4093
Irish Honorary Consulate Palma de Mallorca San Miguel 68 07002 Palma de Mallorca Tel: (0034) 971 722 504	**New Zealand Embassy in Madrid** C/Pinar 7 28006 Madrid Tel: (0034) 915 230 226
South African Embassy in Madrid Claudio Coello 7, 3rd Floor 28006 Madrid Tel: (0034) 914 363 780	**US Embassy in Madrid** Calle Serrano 75 28006, Madrid Tel: (0034) 915 872 200
US Consular Embassy in Palma de Mallorca Edificio Reina Constanza, Porto Pi 8 9D 07015 Palma de Mallorca Tel: (0034) 971 403 707	

Health and Safety

Ibiza is a world-renowned holiday destination that is generally safe for travelers, although there have been incidents of pick-pocketing and purse-snatching, particularly in crowded tourist areas. There is an ongoing worldwide risk of terrorism, and foreigners have been targeted in Spain in recent years. Visitors should be alert to scams, and party in moderation.

There are no compulsory vaccinations necessary before a trip to Ibiza, although precautionary immunizations against hepatitis A and B, typhoid and tetanus shots are often recommended. Visitors should always wear sunscreen and drink lots of water, particularly in the summer. Driving can be hazardous, especially in peak season when the population literally doubles.

Travel Tips

Language

Despite being part of Spain, Catalan is the official language of Ibiza. Most of the population speaks the Castilian form of Spanish, but many locals also know English or German due to the high number of tourists.

Currency

Like the rest of Spain, Ibiza uses the euro (EUR). Currency exchange bureaus, banks or large hotels are the best places to change money, and they will often take travelers' checks as well. Most banks have an ATM, and there are often cash machines at supermarkets. Most purchases should be paid for in cash, although credit cards are commonly accepted at larger establishments.

Time

Ibiza is on the Central European Time Zone, which is one hour ahead of GMT (GMT +1).

Electricity

Ibiza has the same electrical standards as Spain, 50-130 V with Type C and F plug sockets. Travelers should bring a transformer and plug adapter. Most European appliances will work, but those from North America probably will not.

Communications

The dialing code for Spain and the islands is +34. The top mobile operators are Movistar, Vodafone and Amena. Cell phone coverage is good almost all over Ibiza, although the mountainous inland can sometimes experience patchy reception. Phone booths exist, but can be expensive with VoIP internet calling usually a cheaper alternative. Internet cafés are common and affordable.

Duty-free

International travelers arriving from outside the EU may take advantage of the following duty-free allowances: 200 cigarettes or 250 grams of tobacco, one liter of spirits over 22 percent alcohol or two liters of alcoholic beverages under 22 percent, two liters of wine, 50 grams of perfume, 500 grams of coffee, and 100 grams of tea.

Tourist Office

Ibiza Airport Tourist Information Office: +34-9-7180-9118 or http://www.ibiza.travel/en/

Consulates in Ibiza

British Embassy, Ibiza: +34-9-1334-2194

Consulate of Netherlands, Ibiza: +34-9-7130-0450

Emergency

Emergency services: 112

Ibiza chic: its backgrounds, its heritages, and its actualities

From hippy colony to hedonistic playground, the Balearic island has been at the forefront of style for over six decades now...

For anyone who's had the joy of watching the planes fly over DC10, falling asleep on Las Salinas beach or dancing amidst robots in Amnesia, you know Ibiza is a pretty special place. Steeped in a history of hedonistic abandon, for generations the white isle's been a place to let loose to a whole new level, shaped by waves of settlers and clubs that have in turn shaped the fashion of youth culture across the world.

The first modern tourists arrived in Ibiza around 1950, drawn in by rumours of its breath-taking, untouched, natural beauty; an island paradise of stunning seaside coves, clear pure unpolluted waters and picturesque coastlines. Tourism grew and the island prospered and developed. Ibiza was a haven from the political oppression of Franco's Fascist government that ruled Spain from 1936 to 1975, and in the 60s, as the hippie movement spread from San Francisco across the world, a huge number settled in Ibiza, attracted to the cheap rent and rural lifestyle.

It was cemented in 1964 when the Rolling Stones spent a couple of days on holiday in San Antonio. The lack of transport, worries and carefree (and for American's, freedom from conscription) lifestyle were a huge draw for the nascent hippie culture. The staple hippie looks were flares for the boys and crotchet bikinis, headscarves, freckles and little else for the girls.

As the events of 1968 that killed the hippie dream across Europe (from the Prague Spring to continued anti-Vietnam protests to May 68 in Paris) Ibiza became a refuge for hippie's across

Europe, a view reinforced by the 1969 film *More*, by Barbet Schroder, soundtracked by Pink Floyd; it presented Ibiza as a sun-kissed utopia of free love and decadence, with a dark underbelly of drug consumption. A reputation it's never quite shaken.

By the late 70s the disco scene had spread from the African-American gay clubs of Philadelphia and New York across the globe, and had found a second home in Ibiza's hedonistic enclave. Club culture also started to take shape at this point with Amnesia building a loyal following and other discotheques, such as Ku (which later became Privilege) Pacha, Glory's and Lola's drawing in crowds over the Summer months. The spirit of these pre-acid-house moments were captured perfectly by the street photographer Derek Ridgers on a family holiday to the island in 1983; writing later, he spoke of how "at night the streets and bars around the harbour transformed into a hot and heady version of what was happening in London at places like the Camden Palace, The Batcave, Heaven and The Wag... The kind of after hours dance culture which first kicked off in Ibiza balearic beats, ecstasy, superclubs and the rave scene became just about the biggest youth culture story of the late eighties." Revellers wear a lot of white, turbans, leopard print catsuits, capes, peg trousers and string vests. It was a kitschier, sexually promiscuous, beach-to-club metamorphosis of the New Romantic look.

In the 80s the clubs adapted their very basic soundproofing and invested in huge, all-encompassing and powerful sound systems. Disco had evolved alongside the pop music of Bowie and Madonna, and music genres as we know them started to blur into what defined the Balaeric sound; the line is faded between pop and funk, hip hop and early, soulful house sounds coming out of

New York. Free style in mixing is embraced by Alfredo at Amensia and house is about to take over under the magic of open rooftops.

In 1987 British DJs Danny Rampling, Nicky Holloway, Paul Oakenfold and Johnny Walker visited the island and were captivated by the Balearic sound as well as the open-minded atmosphere on the dancefloor. "We were wandering about Amensia," Nicky Holloway reminisced to i-D, "on our first pills, dancing to music that we might have otherwise turned our noses up at. We were there every night after that, thinking, "Fuck, this is it. We've found Narnia!"

They were so inspired that on their return to the UK they launched the club nights Shoom and Spectrum, put the acid into house, and went a long way to creating the dance music scene we enjoy now. At this time British kids were saving up all winter so they could party all summer, dancing alongside off-duty models and transvestites, and wearing dungarees, baggy t-shirts and bucket hats. The loose, androgynous style allowed them the freedom to dance.

In 1989 the Berlin Wall came down, house music went international and sounds poured across borders. On the night of the 22nd of June, 1991, Amnesia opened under new management and thousands of young people invaded the club. This also marked the beginning of the most lucrative time for clubbing with entry and drinks prices steadily increasing as word of acid house spread and its birth sought to capitalise on the Second Summer Of Love. The clubs of Ibiza started to become famous worldwide and the dress code became more commercial; think furry bras in the 90s and cut out swimming costumes in the noughties.

In 1999 the UN proclaimed Ibiza as: "Ibiza, Biodiversity and Culture", a World Heritage City or Patrimony of Humanity, recognising the island as having special cultural or natural significance to the common heritage of humanity. The island reached one hundred thousand habitants and from the 2000s onwards became a party destination for everyone from Calvin Klein to Puff Daddy and George Michael. No longer simply a scene of outsiders pushed aside and left behind by mainstream Europe, Ibiza's legendary party lifestyle has become a global byword for cool, good music and freedom.

Ibiza continues to change and evolve, and while other party destinations and festivals try to steal its crown, the island with its magnetic pull of 24 hour party people take Riccardo Tisci's wild 40th birthday party for example (just look up hashtag #ibiza74) proves Ibiza still manages to be one of the most influential destinations for fashion, style and sound.

The End

www.ingramcontent.com/pod-product-compliance
Lightning Source LLC
Chambersburg PA
CBHW021436080526
44588CB00009B/548